RECYCLING

RECYCLE

The MIT Press Essential Knowledge Series

A Complete list of the titles in this series appears at the back of this book.

RECYCLING

FINN ARNE JØRGENSEN

The MIT Press | Cambridge, Massachusetts | London, England

This book was set in Chaparral Pro by Toppan Best-set Premedia Limited. Printed and bound in the United States of America.

Library of Congress Cataloging-in-Publication Data

Names: Jørgensen, Finn Arne, 1975- author.
Title: Recycling / Finn Arne Jørgensen.
Description: Cambridge, MA : The MIT Press, 2019. | Series: MIT Press essential knowledge series | Includes bibliographical references and index.
Identifiers: LCCN 2019005608 | ISBN 9780262537827 (pbk. : alk. paper)
Subjects: LCSH: Recycling (Waste, etc.)
Classification: LCC TD794.5.J673 2011 | DDC 628.4/458—dc23 LC record available at https://lccn.loc.gov/2019005608

10 9 8 7 6 5 4 3 2 1

CONTENTS

SERIES FOREWORD

The MIT Press Essential Knowledge series offers accessible, concise, beautifully produced pocket-size books on topics of current interest. Written by leading thinkers, the books in this series deliver expert overviews of subjects that range from the cultural and the historical to the scientific and the technical.

In today's era of instant information gratification, we have ready access to opinions, rationalizations, and superficial descriptions. Much harder to come by is the foundational knowledge that informs a principled understanding of the world. Essential Knowledge books fill that need. Synthesizing specialized subject matter for nonspecialists and engaging critical topics through fundamentals, each of these compact volumes offers readers a point of access to complex ideas.

Bruce Tidor
Professor of Biological Engineering and Computer Science
Massachusetts Institute of Technology

If recycling is the answer, what is the question?

Frank Ackerman, *Why Do We Recycle?*[1]

Is there a point to recycling? Does recycling matter? Is it good for the environment? Let me just state right away that it depends. While you may not find that a particularly helpful answer, this book deals with the many ways in which it depends. It is intended as a comprehensive and accessible overview of recycling as an *activity* and a *process* at the intersection of the *material* and the *ideological*. Recycling is not one single thing; it is a broad and sometimes amorphous set of activities that target many different problems, and both problems and solutions change over time and space. The global consequences of recycling are unevenly distributed and are becoming increasingly so.

From a technical point of view, recycling is a series of processes, or an infrastructure, that includes collecting recyclable consumer and industrial materials and products, sorting and processing the recyclables into raw materials, and manufacturing these raw materials into new products. But recycling also has ideological and cultural components. At its core, recycling is about transformation and value, where material waste is turned into potentially useful products. These uses can be both material and ideological. Recycling is one of many concepts that refer to how we might deal with matter about to be discarded. We can reduce, reuse, renew, refuse, recover, repair, restore, or reclaim; each of these represents one way of dealing with waste. All encourage us to rethink our relationship with matter around us. Recycling inevitably draws our attention to the questions: What is waste? What is useful? What is valuable? Who shall be responsible for this transformation? What are the alternatives?

The book is structured as ten short chapters that explore the emergence of recycling as a modern phenomenon and its transformation from a scarcity-driven activity to one predominantly motivated by other concerns, including environmental ideologies and economy. The book is intended to provide an overview rather than a comprehensive survey, and in writing it I have depended on the work of many excellent scholars across the globe. I have particularly relied on the emerging field of *discard studies*, a lively and dynamic field featuring both classic, older works and exciting new scholarship.[2] My background as a historian of technology and environment has also shaped my approach. In this sense, this book is a work of recycling; I have mined the scholarship in order to turn it into something new. Rather than take my book as the final answer, consider it a beginning, as I'm only touching the surface of these much deeper stories.

Recycling inevitably draws our attention to the questions: What is waste? What is useful? What is valuable? Who shall be responsible for this transformation? What are the alternatives?

My work on this book has spanned employment at two different universities: I started the manuscript at Umeå University, Sweden, and completed it at University of Stavanger, Norway, the latter with special support from a Young Excellent Researcher grant that gave me generous funding to spend a month at the Rachel Carson Center for Environment and Society in Munich. Thanks to Christof Mauch for making this stay possible—the book would not have gotten done without it! Dolly Jørgensen also deserves thanks for her support and sharp eye for text that helped me finish the manuscript.

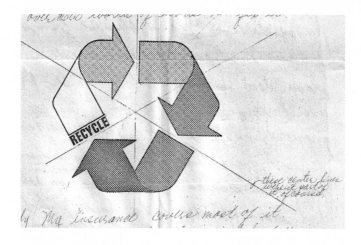

Figure 1 Draft of recycling symbol. Used with kind permission from
Gary D. Anderson.

RECYCLING AS SYMBOL AND AS PROCESS

When the twenty-three-year old architecture student Gary Dean Anderson won a competition to create a symbol to represent and communicate the paper recycling process, he gave shape to an iconic symbol that would come to represent something far more significant in the decades to come. The year was 1970 and environmentalism was a hot topic among students and activists across the world. Only a few months before the competition, Anderson participated in an Earth Day teach-in at University of Southern California. This was the first time Earth Day had taken place, but even then there was a tremendous sense of momentum. On the one hand, Planet Earth was under threat by industrial consumer society. On the other hand, there was rapidly growing engagement from a generation that wanted to reduce its footprint on the planet.[1] Recycling promised to help with both.

The competition was not organized by what most people would recognize as environmentalists, however. Instead, it was the Chicago-based Container Corporation of America (CCA). Founded in 1926, CCA manufactured corrugated boxes, but its CEO Walter Paepcke also had a strong interest in graphic design and the arts. For instance, Paepcke founded the Aspen Institute and hired Herbert Bayer, the Bauhaus designer, to create graphic designs for the Aspen project.[2] Through Paepcke's leadership, CCA amassed a major collection of art that was later donated to the National Museum of American Art. This explains why CCA would be interested in a graphic design competition. But why a competition on recycling?

We need to understand that as a packaging company, CCA actually had a long history of recycling paper. Faced with a pulp shortage caused by the lack of wood (a recurring theme in the history of papermaking, as we will see), Paepcke had turned to recycling paper. At the time of the competition, most of the company's cardboard products came from waste paper. This made good economic sense for the company. More important, packaging had become increasingly visible, both at the point of purchase and after its use and eventual discarding.[3] Companies wanted their products to be as visually attractive as possible, making identification in the store easy and their products irresistible. This proved to be a double-edged sword, however, as more and more packaging ended up on the street and in nature, as litter. The increasing visibility of litter in the late 1960s also made visible the material maker of the litter. The afterlives of products became something companies had to address. CCA felt compelled to address the growing environmental concerns among consumers.

The recycling symbol arose out of the paper littering debate and has grown to become one of the most widely used and recognizable graphic symbols in the world. The design was fairly simple, with three arrows organized in a circle, each one pointing to the next. Each arrow was folded at an angle, as if it were made out of paper. In Anderson's first design, the word "RECYCLE" sat at the base of one of the arrows, but it would eventually be unnecessary. Environmental historian Finis Dunaway argues that the recycling symbol is the most significant visual output of Earth Day, even speculating that it may be one of the most widely seen images in contemporary culture.[4] He is most likely right. I found one variant or other of the recycling symbol on no less than four items within arm's reach of where I am sitting at my desk right now. It is an everyday symbol and an artistic one, even being included in the Museum of Modern Art's permanent architecture and design collection.[5]

The recycling symbol, ubiquitous as it is, sets out to do some heavy lifting. First, it indicates to a product's users that the packaging technically can be recycled. Second, it implies that the product *should* be recycled, and that it is

The recycling symbol arose out of the paper littering debate and has grown to become one of the most widely used and recognizable graphic symbols in the world.

the user's responsibility to make sure the material stays in the loop. Third, it is a signifier of the largely invisible processes of recycling that take place after the consumer leaves the product at a recycling point. This book explores all three aspects of this symbol.

The recycling symbol is simple and elegant, but there is nothing simple or elegant about recycling. Recycling takes us into complex territory, full of both contested symbols and unruly materiality, laden with cynicism and hope, anchored in economy and ecology. Streams of matter, raw and refined, torn from the earth or fashioned from organic matter from eons past, converge, for briefer or longer periods of time, in objects, products, or things, crafted by hand or industrially fabricated, vested in meanings and often subject of controversies. After a period of use, long or short, the individual components separate again into streams. Sometimes this separation is easy, generating new and relatively pure materials. At other times it is hard, where materials have become so intertwined that they resist separation. Such separation processes require technical means, but also social organization and cultural valuation.

Recycling encompasses all parts of this separation process. As sociologist and waste management expert Samantha MacBride argues, recycling is "the most thoroughly developed practice for doing something with solid waste other than burying or burning it."[6] What recycling

The recycling symbol is simple and elegant, but there is nothing simple or elegant about recycling.

aims to do is to close the loop, redirecting streams of matter into something circular that ideally never reaches the waste stage (hence the shape of the symbol).

Recycling aims to eliminate waste; conversely, without waste there is no recycling. But what is waste? We can go to the European Union for one definition: waste is "any substance or object which the holder discards or intends or is required to discard."[7] Such institutional definitions are important for setting international policy goals. While we will see throughout this book how such a definition is somewhat limited, it is also useful in that that it involves not only the discarded matter, but also the one who discards. Furthermore, the act of discarding is not a done deal in this definition—it is potentiality, a process, and ultimately a choice. This openness, the understanding that waste can become *something else*, is critical to understanding recycling. Yet, we also need to understand the larger material and infrastructural contexts in which such choices are seated.

Seen from some parts of the world, recycling seems remarkably efficient at this task. I live and work in Norway, a country that has a highly ambiguous relationship to its own environmental footprint. Norwegians—me included—consume enormous amounts of goods and products from all over the world, paid for by oil money, but we also recycle at record-high rates. Trash is hardly visible in public spaces, and yet we rarely see anyone do anything with waste.[8] It just disappears into high-tech waste management systems.

As we go about our consuming business, matter enters our lives for a period of time, long or brief, before we again part ways. We are of course intimately familiar with this steady progression of matter toward the trash bin, but we rarely look beyond this point. If we look past the trash bin, we can "trouble the assumptions, premises and popular mythologies of waste," as Max Liboiron posits as a goal for discard studies.[9]

Historically, recycling has many origins, all depending on which material we are looking at. The word recycling itself first appeared in the 1920s to designate a cyclic recovery process for liquid chemicals. While recycling as an activity has a much longer history, the word as understood today emerged out of 1960s and 1970s environmentalism, exactly the same stew of actors and concerns from which the recycling symbol emerged.

Currently, recycling is typically seen as a way to achieve a sustainable society, allowing for "the consumption of goods and services that meet basic needs and quality of life without jeopardizing the needs of future generations."[10] It is also an inclusive term, one that presents a way for everyone to do their bit for the environment. As historian Tim Cooper writes, recycling is often perceived as "a modern-day alchemy that can transmute increasing mounds of useless stuff into things of value."[11] Living up to these expectations is not easy. As we will see, the green aura that has surrounded the term since the 1970s is fading away. Some claim that the return of recycling in the postwar years was initially driven by a desire to keep waste out of landfills, which were rapidly filling up. In short, cities were running out of places to dump waste. Others argue that contemporary recycling has an altogether more problematic origin, in the deliberate attempts of business actors to shift responsibility for waste management onto individuals or the public sector.

Whether or not it actually makes a difference, the recycling of waste does give us a window into the processes in which people, societies, and markets ascribe value to materials and actions. This matters because materials matter. As historian Timothy LeCain has argued, "humans and their cultures are *made of and from* matter and cannot logically exist in isolation from it."[12] Waste is not an insignificant part of this matter. Yet, its "global dimension, structure, and flows can only be estimated," writes design scholar Dietmar Offenhuber.[13] Small matter moves around and ends up in places where it shouldn't be, such as small pieces of plastic floating around in the oceans, or a plastic bag stuck in a tree. At some point in time and space, someone made a choice, one that intentionally or unintentionally led to waste being discarded. It is not still, passive, or devoid of action now that we as humans have discarded it. Waste is lively and unruly, escaping containment and classification. We see this all over the planet, on land, in the air, and in the oceans.

Yet people have always sought to tame and control waste. Of course, what counts as waste, and for whom, differs significantly over time. Historian Martin V. Melosi has studied the changing methods for taming waste over 150 years.[14] As he demonstrates, people have placed waste in landfills and dumpsites, in the oceans, and anywhere else they could place it. Another classic work, Joel Tarr's *The Search for the Ultimate Sink*, shows how this search for a final solution for waste is never-ending.[15] Waste does not disappear, but has to be either stored or transformed. Recycling doesn't mean that you get rid of the waste. Instead, recycling gives waste new life. One could see recycling as a recognition *that there is no away*, no final solution for waste. All we can do is try to keep it in the loop and keep it useful.

Waste is constantly on the move. To study it, we can use *following* as a method. This is what researchers do: we follow people and institutions—but increasingly also material things—in an attempt to learn something about the world. We need to follow materials and artifacts—their origins and their destinations—across the planet and over time, with a particular focus on points of transformation and valuation. I have previously called such points *recycling junctions* with reference to Ruth Schwarz Cowan's classic concept, *consumption junction*.[16] It is at the recycling junction that a decision is made—or a habitual behavior is performed—to recycle a product. While many see consumer recycling as an individual action, most modern recycling takes place within large sociotechnical systems and must also be understood in the aggregate form. The act of returning a product for recycling is important, but it is even more important to understand what happens with it afterward. This book will follow materials as they enter into evolving systems and as they move back and forth between producer and consumer, under continual transformation and valuation, in a never-ceasing process toward becoming waste.

Waste is a commodity, to be traded on a global marketplace of buyers and sellers.[17] As waste material moves around the planet, it changes hands many times. One might argue that it isn't fully waste until it stops moving, when someone no longer wants to or is able to handle it. This movement between actors, across distances small and large, is what enables value to be extracted from discarded matter, which is the essence of recycling. These movements can take place inside both informal and formal waste systems. Matter is selected, sorted, evaluated, processed, and resold a number of times, in a process that requires significant labor. All this influences the economics of recycling.

Through the recycling process, the close relationship between labor and waste comes to the forefront. This is perhaps most visible in the act of sorting, which is essential for the movement of materials through recycling infrastructures. Don DeLillo's classic novel *Underworld*, where the main character is obsessed with sorting his own waste, illustrates this point well. In his story, waste becomes a metaphor for American culture. Sorting creates meaning and orders the world. The anthropologist Thomas Hylland Eriksen argues that source separation, the act of sorting waste into different categories, is an acquired skill, a way of converting chaos into order.[18] If recycling is busywork, then this is certainly where most consumers do the work. We invest matter with value through our actions. It can be very labor intensive. At the Rachel Carson Center for Environment and Society in Munich, where I wrote much of this book, a not-insignificant part of the kitchen is taken up by a recycling station where waste can be sorted into four categories (metal, plastic, paper, and other). At home in Norway, we sort out paper, plastic, and food waste from the municipal trash for regular pickup, and also need to take glass and metal to separate recycling stations spread around town. Travel the world and you will see countless such sorting systems, each a front end to a technological system that interfaces with business and the state, local and far away. Waste is not just collected; it must also be processed.

We can find one of the more extreme examples of this in the Japanese town of Kamikatsu, where waste is sorted in no less than thirty-four categories. This small town, located on Shikoku Island, aims to become a zero-waste community and has no garbage trucks. Instead, all residents need to take their own waste to recycling stations. In having such a hands-on approach to recycling, residents get an intimate knowledge of their own waste, learning to recognize and categorize different types of materials. "It can be a pain and at first, we were opposed to the idea," one resident stated to a film team that made a documentary about Kamikatsu.[19] "We are trying to focus more and totally change our lifestyles, to not produce any waste," said a representative from the Zero Waste Academy in the town. The amount of manual labor involved in producing zero waste is high. While many residents were unhappy with the arrangement and the personal hassle it involved, Kamikatsu's Zero Waste initiative also serves as a good example of how involvement in waste management practices through labor confronts people with their own waste production. Kamikatsu finds itself at a recycling junction that can stimulate personal reflection on waste and values.

At its core, recycling is about *transformation* and *values*, where material waste is converted for potentially useful purposes. But what counts as useful? What is valuable? Who shall be responsible for this transformation? What are the alternatives? As we will see in this book, sorting, whether material or cultural, is entirely integral to the process of recycling. It is in the sorting that matter can become waste, or not. What matters is who gets to do the sorting. We know from Geoffrey Bowker and Susan Leigh Star that such forms of classification are thoroughly social activities; in other words, they are shaped by the societies we live in and the values and power relations of these societies.[20]

Recycling has its discontents. There has been considerable debate about the value of recycling in both economic and ideological terms. Some would argue that postconsumer recycling is also a largely symbolic activity, and not an actual solution to whatever problems it is intended to solve. When the journalist John Tierney wrote a 1996 *New York Times* article claiming that "rinsing out tuna cans and tying up newspapers may make you feel virtuous, but recycling could be America's most wasteful activity," a storm of responses flooded in.[21] People are passionate about recycling. Challenging recycling also challenged their acts of caring for the environment. Samantha MacBride would agree with some of Tierney's criticisms, arguing that recycling is busywork that might make us feel like we're doing something environmentally beneficial, but there are many more significant actions that can be taken.

If that is the case, why has recycling remained so popular? Here it might be worth borrowing an explanation from Thorstein Veblen and his concept of conspicuous consumption. To be seen consuming particular products can be an expression of wealth, status, and identity. By extension, philosopher Elizabeth Spelman has argued that wastefulness is an inherent part of conspicuous consumption.[22] Further extending Veblen's concept, one might also talk about *conspicuous recycling*, to be seen (or even seeing oneself) as doing something for the environment through recycling. In the view of many critics, however, we need to go further. Recycling has been portrayed as fundamentally flawed and a distraction launched by an industry that depends on disposability.[23] There is certainly a paradox here.

Recycling is often compared with other environmental initiatives and is found lacking. For instance, the Norwegian researcher Annegrete Bruvoll argues that "we need to recycle plastic for hundreds of years before we have saved the amount of oil we use on a round trip flight between Oslo and San Francisco." Norwegians both travel and recycle a lot, so this comparison strikes home. She argues that environmental attention is too often centered on actions with high symbolic effect and little actual impact: if we don't combine recycling with dramatic lifestyle changes, we are basically hypocrites, because what we actually need to cut is air travel and personal car use.[24] Such comparisons are indeed a challenge for consumers.

There is also a question about the relationship between individual choices and actions versus systems-level impact on large-scale problems. While consumer environmentalism can be seen as a genuine—if perhaps misguided—expression of good intentions, the real waste problem starts elsewhere, with industry and the waste it generates.

Consumers' engagement with their waste often ends at the recycling collection point. What happens with our waste after it leaves our hands, further downstream? This question can be surprisingly hard to answer, as waste is a commodity that gets traded on an increasingly global market. In this process, it gets sorted, separated, combined, and moved around. It shows up in unexpected places. It evades control and moves out of sight. This lack of transparency about what happens with waste after consumer returns is a major challenge when considering the actual effect of recycling. Dietmar Offenhuber argues that access to this information is a requirement for good governance. It is only with this knowledge of where waste goes and what actually happens with it in hand that we can evaluate whether recycling truly is "greenwashing" or worse. He adds, somewhat sarcastically, that while "there is a lack of information about waste systems, there is no shortage of perspectives and opinions about them. The two issues might be related."[25]

In order to build up our governance competence, this book is set up to give an overview of the information we have on recycling and to point readers to where they can go to find out more. We will follow different materials and sets of recycling practices as a way of exploring the many faces of recycling. Each waste type is unique in both upstream consumption and downstream technical processes that lead to recycled material. Through these variations, we will see that recycling is more than just a technical issue. It is deeply embedded in culture, social structure, and economic systems.

ORGANIC WASTE

By the sweat of your brow you will eat your food until
you return to the ground, since from it you were taken;
for dust you are and to dust you will return.

Genesis 3:19

The universe is one big recycling machine. As the late as-
tronomer Carl Sagan stated, "we are made of star stuff."
Everything in us and around us was originally forged
in the heart of a dying star, a very long time ago. From
this star, matter was flung out into the galaxy as the star
went supernova. Eventually, this matter combined into
the world we know today, full of humans, animals, plants,
dirt, water, microbes, cars, airplanes, iPhones, Pokémon
cards, toasters, beer bottles, newspapers, socks, coffee,
and Twinkies. We can call this *stuff*.

All the stuff on Planet Earth comprises a lot of matter. A recent study estimated the total amount of biomass on Earth—or carbon, which is the signature element of life on Earth—at 550 gigatons. Humanity is only 0.06 gigatons of this mass.[1] Another team of scientists calculated the weight of the technosphere—all the structures and things humanity has built—at 30 trillion tons.[2] This is the material we have to work with, at least until humans learn to harvest matter from space.

Recycling is ultimately about life and death, the end of one state of being and the beginning of another one. This is very much the case with organic waste, which is one of the basic forms of matter. The liveliness of the organic character of waste calls out for your attention. Stuff rots. Empty bottles smell. Things converge into messy tangles of things that can't be processed, salvaged, or controlled without first sorting them out, a process that takes labor, skill, judgment, tools, and resources. While the term *waste stream* sounds like something relatively contained, waste is not some orderly collection of matter from which value can be easily extracted. More often than not, we are dealing with wet, oozing, organic waste, bringing the yuck factor into full force. Waste "can touch the most visceral registers of the self—it can trigger responses and affects that remind us of the body's intensities and multiplicities," wrote waste philosopher Gay Hawkins and ethnographer Stephen Muecke.[3] For this reason, contact with waste can be culturally contaminating. One example is the "untouchables" of India, the castes that clean latrines. As Assa Doron and Robin Jeffrey demonstrate in their study of waste management in India, "garbage, refuse, and waste are commonly identified with the *people* who handle them, usually in haphazard, unsystematic ways. To experience waste is ritually polluting, potentially contaminating, and physically risky."[4] The same goes for garbagemen and latrine cleaners in the West. They are not pure and clean. What are the implications for the place of organic waste in the household—and in society?

There's no shortage of organic waste around us: excrement, food leftovers, animal remains, garden clippings, dead leaves falling from trees. Far from dead and inanimate, organic waste decomposes over time, assisted by bacteria and fungus. With proper technique, this process can be assisted in ways that transform organic waste into soil, fertilizer, energy, or heat. This is one fundamental form of recycling.

All times and all places have their own strategies for dealing with organic waste. For instance, one commonly encountered conception of medieval times is how the streets were overflowing with filth and rubbish, with people emptying bedpans from windows, dead animals laying in the gutters, dung piles on empty city lots—and worse. It is easy to imagine the reek and unhealthiness of such cities, and both scholarly works and popular depictions of medieval cities have spread such images of the past. Yet some, like historian Dolly Jørgensen, have challenged such histories, arguing that the recurring regulations targeting urban pollution indicate that excessive waste was seen as a transgression and as offensive to people then as they are to us now.[5] City governments organized regular removal of organic waste generated in stables, kitchens, and latrines. Archaeological finds of streets full of nonorganic garbage could indicate careful leveling of streets under construction, not that the streets were covered in filth. It was only later, with the massive population growth and industrial pollution that came with modern cities, that the urban environment took a dramatic turn for the worse.

Most modern cities have some form of formal or informal services in place to collect and recycle organic waste—it is simply too useful to let it go to waste. Municipal services tend to collect food waste separately, as it can easily be composted to create good soil. Home composting of food and garden waste is also very common. Such composting can be either aerobic or anaerobic, indicating two different strategies of working with the biological decomposition process. Aerobic composting takes place aboveground in open containers that provide air circulation. The access to oxygen allows for a fast and efficient decomposition process, although it might require additional stirring and mixing to bring oxygen to all parts of the compost. Aerobic composting processes generate heat—under the right conditions this can be enough to kill weeds and pathogens, which are a concern in organic waste. Anaerobic decomposition is a completely different beast, as it takes place without oxygen. Such conditions have to be created either underground or in closed containers. The resulting process is not unlike what happens when a stomach digests food, but happens much more slowly. The popular bokashi composting method is one example of an anaerobic process, where kitchen scraps get mixed with a special bacterial starter in a closed bucket. In practice, the waste is fermented, and turns into a mixture that can be used to start other anaerobic composting processes, or it can be added directly to soil or used to make so-called compost tea for watering plants.

Organic waste, including food waste, animal manure, and sewage, can also be transformed to biogas, if allowed to biodegrade under anaerobic conditions. This process creates gases, mostly methane, that can be filtered and burned as an energy source. While most places do this in industrial-sized plants, it is also possible to purchase home biogas systems for small-scale biogas production.

Composting is not the only way of dealing with organic waste. Cultural ideas often shape what people decide to do with it. In Victorian England, for instance, people considered organic waste unhygienic, and cities encouraged people to burn such wastes at home.[6] Later, cities would build large incinerators that could burn this waste in larger quantities. In other times and places, people would keep animals at home or in urban farms to which they could feed food slops and kitchen waste. Historian Heike Weber describes how German cities implemented ambitious source separation systems in the early twentieth century in order to extract food waste, which could make up as much as one fifth of the total waste stream, to feed pigs that could later be eaten.[7] This is also an obvious form of recycling, where waste is turned into meat.

Like so many other forms of recycling, organic waste depends on having intermediaries in place that can not only process the waste, but also ensure that it ends up in the right place. Such intermediaries can be both formal (such as municipal services) and informal (households, scrap dealers, bottle pickers, *kabaadiwala*, and so on). The rag-and-bone trade, which consists of a person who collects household wastes door-to-door, existed somewhere in-between the household and official recycling systems, and helped channel a variety of waste materials to places where they could find new uses. According to Weber, early twentieth century German cities had about one rag-and-bone man or woman per 1,000 inhabitants, typically recruited from the urban poor. Food waste was a considerable part of their trade, allowing such wastes to be put to use as fertilizer, in composting, or for animal food. This demonstrates how food waste is a valuable resource that people in most times and places have been reluctant to throw away. In some places, restaurants would even sell their food waste to rag-and-bone traders. Today, some fast-food chains have begun recycling their used cooking oils into biofuels for its delivery trucks instead of paying to dispose of it.

The generation of food waste has varied greatly over time, however, and this is closely tied to how the skills of dealing with food have shifted. The prevalence of precut and ready-to-cook meals in contemporary society means that much organic waste is removed from food before it even enters the household. In comparison, in earlier times people would buy meat in larger pieces or even slaughter their own pigs and then have to figure out what to do with all of it. Food waste has to a much larger degree become industrial in modern society. This waste is of course put to use in many ways. Behind the scenes in the modern food industry, food is often made in ways that utilize much more of the source than most consumers would. Much of this is highly efficient and perfectly acceptable, although in some cases we cross the line to the gruesomely disgusting, such as mechanically separated meat and boneless lean beef trimmings (also called "pink slime"). Many fast-food companies have stopped using such processes after media coverage and consumer concerns, but whatever else you might think about it, it is a form of recycling that allows for higher utilization of resources.

Changes in food production illustrate how both the composition of the waste stream and people's relationship to waste changed in the postwar period, as consumer society gained momentum. As we will see later on in this book, disposable packaging increasingly replaced reusable types. When precut meats became the standard, households began producing less food waste, but the knowledge and habits that were required to deal with food waste also went out of circulation. Instead, people had to deal with the packaging in which their food and so many other products were delivered. All of these types of waste ended up in one mixed stream for professionals to handle.[8]

Human waste—excrement—has followed a similar trajectory. In modern industrialized society, we rarely need to consider what happens with it, as we have toilets and infrastructures that flush it away for someone else to handle. Historically, this has not been the case. In many European cities, night soil was collected from sites throughout the cities well into the 1950s. Cesspools, privies, latrines, and septic tanks are all examples of off-grid solutions to dealing with human waste. All of these had to be emptied manually by workers, often at night (out of sight, out of mind), after which the waste was transported out of the city or to designated sites for further processing. Handling human excrement still remains a major environmental management problem in many parts of the world. It is not without reason that one of the major initiatives of the Bill and Melinda Gates Foundation is a challenge to re-invent the toilet. Their vision is a hygienic and affordable toilet that functions off the grid, without access to water, sewer, or electrical power.

In 1978, designer and architect Sim Van der Ryn published a manual for how to deal with human excrement at the scale of the individual that became a classic in back-to-the-land and countercultural circuits: *The Toilet Papers: Recycling Waste and Conserving Water*. He explored a variety of scenarios from composting toilets to using ponds of crayfish that can eat excrement before they are themselves eaten for dinner. Van der Ryn took the circular economy challenge seriously, aiming to use recycling to create closed, small-scale loops. "The waste we seek so hard to ignore threatens to bury us," he claimed, echoing many contemporary beliefs of a looming garbage crisis where the sheer mass of waste would overflow the structures we have built to contain them.[9] Van der Ryn's do-it-yourself approach is illustrative of how many approach recycling and waste management in small-scale perspective. This might very well work on an individual level, but the question of scale remains a challenge. How do we bridge the gap between tiny, individually insignificant actions and the immensity of the global environmental challenges the world is facing?

Organic waste accumulates at the edges of our waste management systems. It intrudes, contaminates, and

How do we bridge the gap between tiny, individually insignificant actions and the immensity of the global environmental challenges the world is facing?

evades our control just like many other types of waste. For instance, in the chapter on glass we will see how beverage container recycling is more than a matter of collecting the materials of glass, plastic, and aluminum, which can then be remade into new products because these materials are often mixed with organic waste. Leftover slumps of beverages ferment, spill, and reek, which means that poorly maintained recycling stations will appear as highly unsanitary. In many places, beverage container recycling machines are placed in grocery stores—the point of purchase for most consumers—and the smell of fermenting organic material is not the impression these stores want their customers to have.

Where individual actions and large technical infrastructures meet, friction often arises. In 2017, Thames Water worked to break up a so-called "fatberg," an enormous mass of congealed fat and nondecomposable trash such as diapers and wet wipes, that had blocked the London sewers. Such blockages are not uncommon, as fat, oil, and grease will enter into the sewages through people's sinks, but this one was particularly big, at 250 meters long and weighing 130 tons (equivalent to two Airbus A318 airplanes). It does not sound like much when an individual person cleans up after cooking dinner and ends up rinsing some fat into the sink, but it adds up quickly. Sewage workers equipped with water jets and shovels had to work for weeks to break the fatberg into smaller pieces and take

Where individual actions and large technical infrastructures meet, friction often arises.

it for proper disposal at a recycling plant. A piece of the fatberg was temporarily on display at the Museum of London in 2018, where visitors could watch it slowly change as asperigillus mold started growing on it. Organic waste shows us that "waste" is not just a technical term, but also one that has significant moral dimensions. It is intimately tied not just to our ways of living, but also to our bodies and their metabolism. We produce waste simply by existing. The struggle to deal with this waste never ends.

PAPER TO THE PEOPLE

All history was a palimpsest, scraped clean and
re-inscribed exactly as often as was necessary.
George Orwell, *Nineteen Eighty-four*

If you are reading this book on paper, take a close look at
the page.[1] Hold it up to the light. You'll most likely notice
that the paper is a slightly yellow white, and you can see
that it has a texture—like patches of small fibers. Take
the brightest white copy paper you can find, and you'll see
the same—the seemingly uniform white consists of many
small fibers and has areas that look like it has a higher
density than others. This is paper: tiny shredded cellulose
fibers formed into sheets.

Paper is arguably one of the most central media technologies in history. We use it for storing information and
for communicating with each other across distances, but

also for a whole range of other useful purposes, such as packaging and toilet paper. For all its fragility, paper can be remarkably durable if stored in good conditions. Paper is ubiquitous today, to the point where we more or less take it for granted. It was not always so.

Paper has a long history in which practices of reuse, reclamation, and recycling play a central role in deciding who uses this material and for what uses, as well as what happened with it afterward, motivated by scarcity and lack of resources. In modern times, paper has been anything but a scarce resource, yet paper recycling became one of the flagship activities of the environmental movement in the 1980s. This chapter asks why this happened, introducing some motivations for why people recycle.

Before paper, people wrote on papyrus or parchment. Papyrus, invented in Egypt around 3000 BCE, is the oldest of these technologies. Papyrus is made by taking layers of the papyrus reed (*Cyperus papyrus*), laying them in a woven interlocking pattern and mashing them while soaked in water. The sap from the reed functions as glue, which helps the mashed reeds become sheets that can be glued together as it dries. Papyrus was typically made as scrolls and written only on one side, owing to the way it was fabricated. One side had horizontal fibers that were easy to write on. The other side had vertical fibers, which did not work as well for writing. Scribes still used this side for other things, such as receipts, reminder lists, and so on.

Papyrus could not be made anywhere, however. In the heyday of papyrus use, papyrus reed grew only in the shallow fresh waters of the Nile in Egypt. This gave Egypt a trade monopoly on papyrus. The countries in Asia and in the Mediterranean areas that used significant amounts of papyrus imported it from Egypt.

Parchment was intended as a replacement for papyrus. Parchment is based on prepared animal skins, in particular cows and sheep, which were common throughout Europe. While the preparation of parchment was labor intensive, it could be made more or less anywhere. The apocryphal story is that parchment was invented in the city of Pergamon when Alexandria monopolized the use of papyrus after Pergamon began developing a library to compete with the famed library of Alexandria around 200 BCE.[2] We know from other sources, however, that writing on animal skin is a far older tradition.

In medieval Europe, monasteries were the centers of manuscript production. Here, monks would copy manuscripts for their own libraries or for trade. They were major consumers of parchment. Parchment-making was a resource-demanding trade, where a complete Bible could require skin from up to 200 sheep. As a result, it was not uncommon for monks to both reuse and recycle manuscripts. The old text would be scraped or washed off and would often be visible under the new writing. One can debate whether such medieval manuscript practices should be called recycling or reuse, as the ways in which manuscripts were broken down and reconstructed featured some parts of both.

With paper, however, recycling came into full force. Papermaking represented a set of knowledge that slowly moved across continents. Paper had been invented in China as early as 100 BCE. Mark Kurlansky writes that Europeans had known about the existence of paper for a long time before they actually started using it.[3] It was not until the widespread adoption of Arab mathematics and expanding literacy that paper came to replace parchment in the West. In Europe, paper began replacing parchment from the early fifteenth century, although parchment remained popular for quite some time.[4] Paper was much cheaper than both papyrus and parchment.

Paper is made from cellulose fibers from broken-down wood or fabric, diluted in water, and passed over a screen until it weaves and forms a sheet, which then can dry. Cellulose is a common organic compound that can be found in plants all over the world. As a result, many different substances can be used to make paper. Early paper consisted of mulberry bark, hemp, and rags that were mixed with water, mashed into pulp, pressed, and left in the sun to dry. The basics are not particularly difficult; when visiting the Suho Paper Memorial Museum in Taipei a few years ago, I got to make my own paper, for instance. To make high-quality paper requires adequate raw materials, lots of water, and good molds.

The development from papyrus to parchment to paper is not quite linear, but one clear trend we can see is that the raw material necessary for production becomes more and more easily accessible. This has to do with price and quantity, but also geography and geopolitical control over resources.

The introduction of new technologies often influences people's recycling practices. Book historian Erik Kwakkel has documented how, after Gutenberg, when handwritten books became obsolete, book binders dismantled old books to reuse the parchment in bindings. This gave the books a second life, he argues, where fragments survive until today, to be studied by scholars.[5] Manuscript fragments have also been found in medieval dresses, as tailors were drawn to parchment for the same reasons as book binders.[6] Parchment was durable and stable, and it could provide structural support. This makes many medieval books palimpsests, where former uses are visible underneath current ones.

While the term recycling did not exist in medieval times, people certainly engaged in acts of reuse and recycling as an expression of scarcity. For instance, as medieval historian Robin Fleming has argued, in early medieval Britain the reuse and recycling of Roman ruins was a common practice. Medieval buildings are also palimpsests, often consisting of scavenged materials from earlier structures.

With papermaking, however, we are definitely talking about recycling in the true meaning of the word. First, papermaking itself represents a form of recycling. The first British white papermills that could reliably produce high-quality paper for writing or printing were built near Dartford in the late sixteenth century.[7] These mills were completely dependent on a reliable supply of rags (typically worn-out linen cloth) that could serve as the cellulose base for paper. For this purpose, the mill's owner, John Spielman, was granted a monopoly for buying and dealing in rags. Making paper from these rags was time-consuming and labor-intensive. The rags had to be prepared and cleaned before they were softened through fermentation for a whole month. They could then be shredded and mixed with water to form pulp.

In the mid-1600s, Dutch papermakers invented a new way of turning rags into pulp using a mechanical, bladed beater. The Hollander beater, as it was called, allowed linen rags of different qualities to be mixed. The paper made from this process was much cheaper than other paper, and with experience the quality of the paper improved as well.[8] The rags, no matter how dirty, were broken down into individual components, and reassembled into a new product. The Hollander, which arrived in America in the mid-1700s,

While the term recycling did not exist in medieval times, people certainly engaged in acts of reuse and recycling as an expression of scarcity.

could be powered by either windmills or waterwheels, and could replace several workers.[9]

With increased production capabilities, the demand for rags only grew, but the supply did not increase at the same rate. By the end of the eighteenth century, Britain imported 3,405 tons of foreign rags for its paper-making industry, mostly from Scandinavia and the continent.[10] In the eighteenth and nineteenth centuries, paper manufacturers needed to establish a system of rag collection before they could start a paper mill. This is why so many of the early mills were located close to big population centers such as Philadelphia, Boston, and New York. In 1769, newspaper readers in Boston could read a notice saying that "the bell car will go through town about the end of each month to collect rags."[11] William Rittenhouse (1644–1708), trained in Germany, founded America's first paper mill in what is now Philadelphia in 1690. As in European paper mills, this mill used discarded rags of cotton and linen to make paper. After the American Revolution, American paper mills could not meet the demand for paper and they had serious problems finding enough rags. In 1776, the Massachusetts House of Representatives declared that "the Inhabitants of the Colony are hereby desired to be very careful in saving even the smallest quantity of Rags proper for making Paper."[12] American paper mills had to import rags from Europe to meet demand. There's nothing new about waste being shipped between continents.

Material shifts influenced the rag trade. European textile mills began using more and more wool instead of linen or cotton in the eighteenth century, and wool rags did not work for papermaking. So papermakers started looking for alternative materials to use. Asbestos paper never took off (which was probably not a bad thing), nor did potato paper, nor straw paper, just to mention some of the materials they experimented with. Matthias Koops (1776–1812) was a papermaker, born in Pomerania but working in England, who experimented with many such ragless papers. In 1800, he published *Historical account of the substances which have been used to describe events, and to convey ideas, from the earliest date to the invention of paper*, a book that was simultaneously a historical survey of substances used in papermaking and an experimental publication, to solve the supply problem by finding a reliable way to make paper without rags. From his base at the Neckinger Mill in London, Koops developed what we can call true recycling of paper. He patented a process for "Extracting Ink from Paper and Converting Such Paper into Pulp" on April 28, 1800. The second edition of his book, published in 1801, was experimentally printed on recycled straw paper, probably the first use of recycled paper in the West, and contained an appendix printed on paper made from wood, supposedly the first use of bleached wood paper in an English book.[13]

In the end, it was not straw, but wood that came to be the main source for paper manufacturing. Wood is about 50 percent cellulose and requires significant treatment in order to be usable for paper. Discovered by the French chemist Anselme Payen in 1838, cellulose gradually became more common in papermaking from the mid-1800s. This led to the rise of the modern paper industry, with all the mechanization and industrialization that this implied, as described in Judith McGaw's classic history of the industrial revolution in the paper industry, *Most Wonderful Machine*.[14]

With industrialization and large-scale paper production, paper use increased dramatically. The rise of the newspaper in the mid-1800s contributed greatly to this development, and newspapers were completely dependent on a steady supply of cheap paper. Paper recycling was an integrated part of this new industry. Many cities started municipal recycling programs to extract paper from the waste stream for this purpose. For instance, Baltimore started such programs in 1874 and New York in 1896. As historian Susan Strasser argued, dealing with garbage in this way was something relatively new. As more and more paper moved through the household, it had to be integrated into the waste management routines. Strasser describes how in 1882, a household economy manual for children had to define what a wastebasket was: "It is for collecting all the torn and useless pieces of paper, and should be emptied every day, care being taken that nothing of value is thus thrown away."[15] This shows how household waste management practices are both skills and habits that have to be cultivated.

Yet paper cannot be endlessly recycled. As paper is broken down into cellulose again, the fibers get shorter and less flexible. The resulting paper is of lower quality than new paper and is best suited for things like cardboard or paper towels. While paper can theoretically be recycled up to nine times, the presence of inks, clays, and glues in practice reduces that number to four times in the twenty-first century.[16] As a result of this steady degradation, recycled paper products are often associated with lower quality, somehow being tainted or reduced.

Paper can be created in various qualities. For instance, as medieval historian Hannah Ryley writes, the willingness "to use resources of variable quality was just one of the many ways in which material was conserved in the fifteenth century."[17] But as the printing and papermaking industry developed, early modern printers and consumers eventually got obsessed with making paper as white as possible through a variety of techniques, including "souring" or fermenting, until bleach was discovered by the chemist Charles Tenant in 1799. Whiteness became a signifier of high quality—and this idea remains with contemporary paper. Of course, not all paper needs to be of the same high quality: newspapers depend on low-grade and cheap paper and packaging is rarely of high-grade paper. The brown coffee filters many of us use are a common example of unbleached paper, as are cardboard and brown wrapping paper. These types of papers are easier to create with recycled fibers.

Raw material supplies greatly influence the motivations for recycling. During World War II, resource scarcity struck large parts of the world. In times of scarcity, people can be more willing to accept products of lower quality or to endure potential contamination of proximity to waste. The war effort required material, established trade networks became difficult, and a shortage of workers meant that priorities had to change. In England, paper became a scarce resource after access to wood pulp was cut off with the Scandinavian occupation. This was no trivial matter. Paper was one of the most strategically important materials during World War II, writes historian Peter Thorsheim. While it wasn't as important as steel, rubber, or petroleum, paper still was necessary for "propaganda posters, bullet cartridges, shipping containers, and radio containers."[18]

The British turned to *salvage* as a means of finding new sources of cellulose, encouraging citizens to save all kinds of paper at home for the war effort. This was still not sufficient, so the government turned its attention to other kinds of paper, such as books, business correspondence, personal papers, and government records—of which there

Raw material supplies greatly influence the motivations for recycling.

were vast quantities in Britain, in private homes, in businesses, and in government offices. Hundreds of millions of books were contributed to the war effort as recyclable material, writes Thorsheim.[19] These obviously weren't worthless or waste.

War and other extreme situations change the way people think about waste and value. As Tim Cooper has argued, waste went from being seen as worthless to being a valuable resource during World War II.[20] Preserving it and putting it to new use through salvage became an act of patriotism and citizenship, even if that meant recycling paper that would otherwise not be seen as waste, such as "rare books and manuscripts whose value, many believed, was far greater than the paper on which they were written."[21] Needless to say, such extreme recycling could not be maintained after the war. The Britons were scrapping their cultural heritage, their national memory, for making new paper for the war effort. This was not culturally or materially sustainable. For many, the end of the war and the return of freedom meant that one could stop recycling.

Paper recycling did not, however, stop after the war, as used paper could so easily be used in the production of new paper. Historian Ylva Sjöstrand's study of waste management in postwar Stockholm gives us an idea of the many different actors that were involved in the paper recycling business. Motivated by a high price for paper, the paper industry itself was a major driver for re-use and recycling at the time. The industry continuously sought to improve processes and technological solutions for cleaning print off paper.[22] With the increasing use of packaging of consumer goods in the 1950s, return paper use increased considerably in Sweden, when the two largest buyers of paper started making cardboard of mixed return paper. They built up an infrastructure for waste paper collection, replacing the older, informal collection system that was primarily handled by scrap dealers.[23] The Stockholm municipal services sorted paper (and rags) out of communal waste stream and sold it, but there was also extensive paper collection organized outside of the municipal services.[24] Volunteer organizations collected paper waste in Stockholm and sold it for recycling. A large network of formal and informal collectors contributed to bringing paper back for recycling. In 1964, Sweden had what was considered the most advanced return paper facility in Europe, and could export waste paper to other countries.[25]

Today, paper recycling is primarily a way of dealing with an excess of paper. Paper is ubiquitous, to the point where our houses and our offices are overflowing. In the digital age, paper is hardly going away. According to the US EPA, paper is, by weight, the largest part of the recycling stream, except for steel. Paper is everywhere in public spaces and in nature as well. What to do with it all?

These questions became more pressing in the 1970s, as paper consumption reached new heights and the nascent environmental movement gathered strength. In the 1980s, paper recycling became a way of backing up claims of greenness. If you claimed to be an environmentalist but didn't use recycled paper, you were a hypocrite. The act of sorting and returning household paper waste and then seeing it return in the form of recycled paper illustrates the loop that recycling is intended to close. In that sense, the appeal of paper recycling is easy to see.

While commonly seen as an environmentally beneficial practice, paper recycling is not unproblematic from an environmental point of view. The recycling process creates toxic and hard-to-dispose-of sludge and requires massive amounts of water. While it requires less water than virgin papermaking, one should not forget that virgin papermaking is "one of the most environmentally harmful industries on earth," according to Elizabeth Royte.[26] Using less paper in the first place would be more environmentally friendly than any paper-making process.

The term palimpsest, taken from manuscript studies, is useful for thinking about how recycled materials tell us something about both matter and society. A palimpsest designates a page from which the original text has been removed so that the page can be reused. A critical feature of the palimpsest is that it still wears visible traces of its earlier form. Recycled materials are also palimpsests, although the traces can be hard to see. Most often this takes the form of a subtle or not-so-subtle degradation of the quality of the material, which is why some use the term *downcycling*. Few materials can be recycled infinitely (although glass and aluminum are good candidates). Paper is an example of a finite recyclable because the fibers get shorter and shorter with each reprocessing. The recycling process also has its own environmental cost. In short, recycling is no panacea.

RAGS TO RICHES

Sellers and buyers were anxiously speculating on the amount of profit to be realized from these large, somewhat dirty-looking bales, and visions of filthy rags being transmitted into shining gold rose up before them.

Samuel Jubb, *A History of the Shoddy Trade* (1860)

"For the apparel oft proclaims the man," Polonius advised his son Laertes in William Shakespeare's play *Hamlet*. Clothes make the man, we say in modern English, but the advice is timeless. Of all human belongings, few are as personal as clothes. Clothes protect us from the environment, they hide—or flaunt—our bodies, they signal belonging in social groups, and they serve as means of expression. Clothes of some kind are as old as humanity. Recent studies indicate that clothes allowed humans to migrate north from Africa into cooler climates, some 70,000 years ago.[1] Clothes made man in more ways than one.

Juliet B. Schor has pointed out how throughout most of human history, clothing has been expensive.[2] Making clothes is time intensive, labor intensive, and resource intensive. Raw materials have to be turned into cloth, which can then be fashioned into clothing. All this requires appropriate skills and tools. As a result, few people could afford many sets of clothes. Instead, people took care of their clothes, through mending, repairing, and adapting. Clothes were to be used for as long as possible. The anthropologist Arjun Appadurai has described the social life of clothing, in which a set of clothes would have a long life with a series of uses, often beginning as formalwear for special occasions, and then become everyday wear, before it becomes suitable for home use only.[3] In the end, the clothing becomes rags, which as we have seen were once critical to the papermaking trade.

Even discarded clothes have value. Ragpickers, scavengers, *chiffoniers*, and rag-and-bone men invested significant labor in their trade, which was to extract rags from the waste stream and pass it on up the value chain. They scoured the cities looking for rags that could be sold, searching streets, alleys, and dustheaps. Most precious were rags that were clean, white, and made of linen, although ragpickers—most often women—would collect any color rag, writes sociologist Martin O'Brien.[4] In

Victorian dust-yards, which were often centers of rag-sorting labor, women would wade through trash, sorting and sifting.[5] This was—and can still be—dangerous work, as dirty rags could be unhygienic and potentially infectious. During the Napoleonic wars in the early 1800s, scavengers would go through the battlefields, stripping dead soldiers of uniforms that could be sold to papermakers. This also happened at Gettysburg in 1863, although not without controversy and protests against disrespectful behavior.[6]

Prior to the industrial revolution, clothes were scarce—not in the sense that few people had clothes, but that an excess of clothes was considered a luxury. But textile production was one of the engines of the industrial revolution. Around the beginning of the nineteenth century, the British textile industry was in flux. Wool was still dominant, but cotton fabric would soon replace it as the most important textile. The older cottage industry, or household manufacturing, system soon gave way to industrialized factory production. We have already seen how the shift from linen to wool in the textile industry drove paper manufacturers to search for a replacement raw material. The shift from wool to cotton would drive other changes since the industry generated other raw materials that were not just recycled, but also traded for profit.

While the British landscape is well suited to raising sheep, the rapidly expanding textile industry required more raw materials than the domestic market could provide. Wool for the textile mills would come in from the whole British empire, including Australia and New Zealand, as well as South America. One type of woolen fabric that grew in prominence as the textile industry expanded was *shoddy*. Shoddy is a textile material that was produced from the early 1800s using old woolen rags and textile mill leftovers.[7] Demand for shoddy came from wars and professionalization of militaries: Shoddy became material for uniforms, writes media scholar Hanna Rose Shell.[8] A wide range of other cloths were produced from shoddy, such as "Flushings, Druggets, Paddings, Duffels ... Mohairs, Pilots, Tweets, Peterhams," lists Samuel Jubb, historian of the shoddy trade.[9]

The story of shoddy production has all the elements familiar to recycling scholars. The production requires sorting and processing, much of which is manual labor. Shredding the raw material for shoddy created dust that caused sickness among the workers. No wonder that shoddy's nickname was "the devil's dust." When Friedrich Engels toured England in 1844, he visited the textile industry and saw firsthand the misery among the workers. We also recognize the cultural connotations that the word "shoddy" has taken on, as something of low quality and inferior compared to "virgin" material.[10] Jubb clearly writes in defense of the shoddy industry, where "goods of an uneconomical character have been put upon the market, and the effect has rebounded to the injury of the reputation of the manufacture."[11] Old clothes have become material to be traded throughout the history of textile recycling, even if sellers of clothes have often had a low social status. As Samuel Jubb describes the sellers, "In the early stages of the rag and shoddy trade, the calling of a rag merchant was scarcely considered 'respectable,' and men of capital and 'standing' held aloof. They left it in the hands of the small capitalists, and well did they use their opportunity."[12] Shoddy's reputation for low quality was not deserved, he argued—it just needed to be put to appropriate purposes: "Let not the world suppose that shoddy is execrable rubbish, which it is almost felonious to use in the fabrication of cloth, nor let it entertain the idea that shoddy goods, (so called,) are not composed largely of sheeps' wool as well as shoddy."[13]

With the industrial revolution, clothes became a consumable item that eventually would become waste. Susan Strasser shows how between 1880 and 1930 Americans began to produce trash at a scale that was unprecedented. In the course of the twentieth century, the price of clothes dropped: in 1918, an average of 16.6 percent of the annual expenditures of an American family was spent on clothing, but this rate dropped steadily over the century, until it was only 4.2 percent in 2002–2003, yet people have more and more articles of clothing.[14] The falling annual expenditures was not because people stopped buying clothes but

Old clothes have become material to be traded throughout the history of textile recycling, even if sellers of clothes have often had a low social status.

because the price per article went down. People—at least many of them—no longer needed to wear their clothes until they fell apart, nor did they buy clothes only a few times every year. Discarding clothes became easier as their value plummeted.

Clothes are no longer a rare or valuable product. Western consumers in particular have a wealth of clothes, with bulging wardrobes and drawers and walk-in closets. More and more people have clothes for any occasion. Clothes are as aspirational as ever, allowing us to dress for success and for the people we want to be (after all, clothes make the man). But at the same time, many articles of clothing are worn less than ever.

Environmental historian Adam Rome describes the global fashion industry as "creative destruction," invoking Schumpeter's classic thesis.[15] As Schumpeter argued, capitalism is dependent on the constant devaluation or destruction of current wealth in order to create new wealth. This constant cycle of destruction and production is an inherent feature of the society we live in, but it is no closed loop. Fashion operates after these principles and "is now central to a global economy that is unsustainable," Rome argues. He is not alone: Sociologist Juliet B. Schor has called this "fast fashion," similar to fast food—convenient, low-quality, and easily forgettable.[16] Clothes are a product of a global industry that has growth as the most important goal, "made possible by a faster cycling of raw materials, products, finance and even social meanings."[17] Making clothing has huge environmental costs. Cotton is water intensive, for instance. Polyester production leads to dangerous emissions and is energy intensive. Furthermore, in such an economy, there are few barriers to discarding clothes.

Obsolete and discarded clothes do not have to go directly in the trash, though. As consumers, we are encouraged to recycle our clothes, or at least send them to the second-hand marketplace. In this way, we can prevent the manufacturing of new clothes. Such initiatives are often run by charities, such as Goodwill, the Salvation Army, or Oxfam.[18] In Norway, most collection containers in recycling stations have been carefully secured against theft. This is not just because the contents have value, but because people have gotten trapped inside the containers in the attempt to steal clothes.

The used clothing trade is not insignificant. By volume, it is one of the most significant US exports, for instance. Most used clothing gets shipped abroad. The anthropologist Lucy Norris, who has followed the global clothes trade closely, argues that while clothes recycling allows consumers to think of themselves as engaging in ethical behavior, there is no significant ethical impact on the market exchanges the clothes go through in their second life.[19] The intentions and values of the clothes' former owners are inevitably sheared away from the clothes, as they move through "global value networks that skirt regulation and co-opt public officials, politicians, corporate capital, NGOs and chains of traders and petty hawkers" that are largely undocumented.[20] Like paper recycling, textile recycling is both moral and material, often starting out with charitable intentions but ending with sheer economic motivations "in informal street markets in the poorest parts of the world."[21]

The second-hand clothes trade is now international, with clothes typically moving from the Global North to the Global South. Norris has traced the social and economic impact of the clothes trade. In India, the trade happens with a network of "dealers that negotiate the borders between the legal and the illegal, the formal and informal."[22] As we will see with other materials, this is not an uncommon setup when waste is involved.

What happens with second-hand clothes and where do they go?[23] The short documentary *Unravel* gives us a compelling glimpse into the world of clothes recycling.[24] The documentary takes place in Panipat, north of New Delhi. Here, truckload after truckload of clothes from the Global North roll in every day, having first been brought to India on cargo ships. On arrival, they go through customs, in vacuum-packed plastic bales. Here, the clothes are slashed by women workers with circle saws, to "protect the clothes from theft." The slashing is a significant part of the recycling process, as it is through this action that the clothes can no longer be reused as clothing. It is the beginning of a process where the added cultural value of brand names, design, looks, and so on has to be stripped away from the material. It is no longer clothing, but just raw material to be recycled.

After shredding, the clothes need to be sorted in different colors. Imagine laundry day at home, just on an industrial scale. This requires space, so big courtyards and warehouses become an important resource. The slashed and sorted clothes then get bundled up again and go to Panipat for further processing, a task for men. Here, buttons and zippers and sequins that can't get recycled get cut off, something that is again women's work. Then the clothes get cut up even more to prepare for the shredding machines. The rag machine tears the clothes up, and then the teaser machine shreds it even further. The card machine turns it all into sheets of shoddy that the spinning machine turns into thread. And then, finally, blankets are woven from the thread. This more complex machinery is handled by men, illustrating how the labor is gendered. The blankets then get shipped back to the West, closing the recycling loop.

Norris's work explores and documents the labor system that we see glimpses of in *Unravel*. She describes how a system of migrant workers and subcontractors leads to both labor and environmental problems. There is also a substantial black market in clothes that are not shredded, but sold.[25] There are many ways for waste to evade control, to shift between categories. What this shows is that there is nothing simple about what happens with textiles.

Textile recycling, like so many other types of recycling, is dependent on a periphery that can absorb and process the waste from the center. This is a relatively new phenomenon in a global context. Doron and Jeffrey describe how the Indian *kabaadiwala*, "the equivalent of the British rag-and-bone man, who bought household discards to resell," used to trade in textiles—both cloth and old clothes—but since people rarely threw away clothes, it was never a major item.[26] In India, however, this changed over the last thirty years, with imports of clothes from the West.

Perhaps the most fascinating part of the *Unravel* documentary is the meeting between Indian workers and Western clothes, and how they imagine the people who used—and discarded—these clothes might be. In the interviews with the women who worked with the clothes they point out how "the first time anyone comes here, they always ask where have all these clothes come from?" Their theory is that the clothes are coming here, virtually unworn, because of a water shortage in the West. So people throw away clothes instead of washing them. They are not sure, but they certainly don't understand it. The casual discarding of unused clothes is a mystery to them, something that needs to be explained. While their suggested answers are perhaps not the best, the underlying question

Textile recycling, like so many other types of recycling, is dependent on a periphery that can absorb and process the waste from the center.

is a good one: why is this flood of virtually unworn clothes coming from the West?

Clothes make the man, but in the end, men and women unmake the clothes. The question is, do we have any options than unmaking clothes? Most research recognizes that the vast overproduction of disposable clothes is a major problem. This is a problem that recycling can't solve, it can only mitigate some of the symptoms. And, of course, recycling generates even more problems. Buying less, buying better, and taking better care of clothes through repairs and mending would be some ways to reduce this overproduction. There is no need to recycle waste that isn't generated in the first place. This brings us to another aspect of the labor involved in dealing with waste. There's a transformation in recycling that requires not only resources, but also resourcefulness and skills.

In order to get to this point, we need to reconsider the place clothes have in our lives. Clothes, like all things, are invested with meaning through their use. We all have some clothes that we have had for ages, and that have some kind of special affective value beyond the monetary. Or they can just be very comfortable. For instance, I have a Nike hoodie sweater that I've had for more than twenty years and that I regularly put on. It hardly shows any signs of wear, so it must be of surprisingly good quality to have lasted that long. But I can also wear out a pair of pants in three months. How can we move away from disposable clothes to deeper, more meaningful relationships with the clothes we use?

We can take some lessons from design history on how some clothes companies have sought alternative relationships with their consumers. Take, for instance, the sports brand Patagonia, which was established by the climber Yvon Chouinard in 1973. Chouinard was an elite "dirtbag" climber who started to produce equipment for people like himself. Patagonia aimed to establish a completely different identity than most other brands. The company wanted to explore the meaning of what extreme sportswear could be. I don't think I am alone in wearing clothes branded as extreme sportswear to walk the dogs in light rain, but in the case of Patagonia's founder, the term had an actual meaning; before it had been just another marketing tool. For Patagonia, signaling a distance from the inherent obsolescence of fashion was important.[27] As fashion historian Michelle Labrague writes, "Just as fashion has the capacity to define the self, [Patagonia's] athletic clothes allow for transformation."[28] This transformation is not just one of the relationship between clothes and user, but also between producer and the surrounding world of waste and resources. Slow, rather than fast, fashion is one way forward.

In recycling, all such concerns about use-value and emotional value get stripped away. There is only color and material. Through reuse and repair, we can keep some of this meaning (or invent new meaning). Textile recycling illustrates how materials can feed into both private and industrial recycling processes, as well as what might be termed informal recycling systems and business-driven systems. With the expansion of trade infrastructures, textile recycling has gone from a local to a global process, where materials are shipped from the West to low-cost countries in Asia and Africa, where they are processed and turned into new materials (such as shoddy) or re-purposed before being shipped back to the West or other destinations.

GLASS AND CLASS

I'll send an SOS to the world

I hope that someone gets my

Message in a bottle

The Police, "Message in a Bottle," 1979

The glass bottle is the oldest form of beverage container still in use. We don't know exactly where, when, or how glass as a material originated, but people have been able to produce glass for at least 5,000 years. The Romans perfected the glass bottle as a beverage container for wine as early as the second century CE. Glass is made by combining sand, soda ash, and limestone, which is then mixed with so-called cullet—crushed glass—and heated up to 1,500 degrees Celsius.

Until the early 1900s, bottles were hand-blown from molten glass, which meant that production was labor intensive and bottles were expensive and all slightly different. The automatic, industrial bottle production that gradually took over from the beginning of the twentieth century coincided with—and enabled—significant shifts in the distribution and consumption of bottled beverages. At this time, when the modern beverage industry took shape, one of the main logistical challenges was how to package beverages to get them safely to the consumer. This was a new phenomenon; previously, beverages were often consumed at the point of purchase, in bars or from drink fountains.

Standardized and industrially produced glass bottles became the solution. Originally invented by the Swedish bottler Anders Bjurholm and cork cap factory owner Gustaf Emil Boëthius in the 1880s, mass-produced identical glass bottles could be sold in large quantities.[1] While cheaper than hand-blown bottles, they were still expensive, so the bottlers needed to use them several times to keep beverage prices down. The way they managed this was to set a deposit on the bottles, where the consumer paid an extra sum when buying the beverage, to be refunded when the bottle was returned. The bottler would then clean the bottle, refill it, and send it out again. In this way, a single bottle could be refilled dozens of times, forming a closed loop between bottler, distributor, and consumer. In the United States, breweries still claimed ownership of their bottles and created distinctive bottle designs. In Norway, most breweries had agreed to use standardized bottles since 1906, which meant that they could reuse each other's bottles. Other than the contents, the glued-on label was the only thing that distinguished one brewery's bottles from another.

The reusable deposit glass bottle had much in common with a library book. The consumer did not buy the bottle, but was only borrowing it from the bottler. The bottles were part of a shared infrastructure of bringing beverages to the market, generally organized by the bottlers' trade organizations. Nonstandard containers such as the iconic and distinctively shaped Coca-Cola bottles, also carried deposits, but were not interchangeable in the same way.[2] American bottlers often embossed their bottles with logo and name as a means of claiming ownership. This practice built on older traditions, where British inns and pubs would emboss their bottles as early as the 1700s. Historian Robert Friedel writes about how, at the end of the nineteenth century, bottlers marked their bottles with "This bottle to be washed and returned" and "This bottle not to be sold," but it was still a challenge for them to collect enough of their bottles after use.[3] This is, of course, technically not recycling; it is reuse. But the model that was established—the deposit-refund system—became very influential for later recycling systems.

The reusable deposit glass bottle had much in common with a library book. The consumer did not buy the bottle, but was only borrowing it from the bottler.

Consumers did not always return bottles as intended. While few would throw away or break the bottles, they could be reused in other ways. For instance, every year during the fruit-harvesting season, Scandinavian bottlers faced shortages of their shared, standardized bottles. The reason: housewives chose to use these bottles for their homemade fruit syrup. While the bottles were technically the bottlers' property, as the bottlers would frequently remind their customers in newspaper announcements at such times, consumers had their own ideas of what the value of these bottles was. While the bottles were not wasted, this subversive reuse limited the efficiency of the industrial systems that depended on their remaining in the loop. Other consumers would use the bottles for storing kerosene for lamps for a while, before returning the bottle at a later point for the refund. Bottlers needed to develop solutions for detecting such bottles, which would require special cleaning before they could be reused. In practice, this meant that a woman had to smell each incoming bottle.

Despite all these limitations, the bottle return system worked well enough within the particular business model from which it emerged. Return rates were high, indicating that a majority of bottles were reused. Their value was in their bottle-ness, so to speak. In his environmental history of Coca-Cola, Bart Elmore writes that soft drink bottles had a return rate of about 96 percent in 1948. At this time, Coke bottles were reused twenty-two times on average. As he says, "putting a price on trash made people waste less."[4]

Bottlers sorted and washed the bottles, a process that required labor and water and that generated some environmentally harmful wastes. Bottlers had to make major investments in building an infrastructure, with bottles, crates, transportation, collection, storage, and cleaning, but could lower the retail prices of beverages. For the consumer, much of this infrastructure was invisible. Such a system carried considerable technological momentum, to use historian of technology Thomas P. Hughes's term.[5] Sunk costs in particular infrastructures influence the willingness to adopt alternative solutions, until the economic advantages of doing so are too big.

Despite the strong momentum, the deposit-refund system came under significant pressure in the postwar years. The whole brewery sector was in rapid transition, in which prewar business models were challenged by new ones. New materials, new beverage containers, and new distribution networks all challenged the economic logic that underpinned the bottlers' deposit-refund system. Glass bottles became cheap enough that bottlers did not have to reuse them. And since they didn't have to be reused, they could be much thinner and lighter, too, enabling transport over larger distances for lower costs. With longer transportation distances, the bottlers definitely didn't want the bottles back. The loop could no longer be taken for granted. The beverage container was no longer a valuable resource and the disposable society was just around the corner. This development shaped the way beverage containers were handled and understood in significant ways, but the process of substituting reusable bottles with new disposable containers did not happen without resistance.

The "No deposit, no return" bottle launched in the 1950s. These bottles were novelties, being described as "bottles that were sold along with the beer."[6] They were a response to cheap canned beverages—first tin, but later aluminum; we shall return to aluminum in the next chapter. Glass producers met the can competition with one-way glass bottles that, according to advertisements, could just be thrown away after use. And people did throw them away, to the point where disposability became a symbol of progress and modernity, as Vance Packard would argue in his 1960 book *The Waste Makers*.[7]

The one-way beverage containers changed bottles from reusable to recyclable, and this move is significant. The value in bottles, then, was reduced to the raw material—glass that could be crushed, melted, and again turned into new bottles or other glass products. This represents a clear shift in the understanding of the way we value bottles. However, being recyclable is no guarantee of actual recycling.

Reusable glass bottles are in and of themselves not more—or less—environmentally friendly than one-way containers. This is another case of "it depends." Reusable glass bottles are heavy, which means that transportation requires more energy and leads to more pollution. This, however, becomes a significant problem only when bottlers start shipping their products over long distances. Cleaning the bottles also requires water and energy, and creates caustic waste water. Disposable containers are lighter and easier to handle during transportation over long distances and from shop to home. Early one-way containers were advertised to women as easier to carry home, as they were the ones doing the shopping.

Despite the inherent recyclability of the glass, disposable bottles were marketed as one-way bottles that did not need to be returned. American consumers in particular eagerly latched on to these new practices. As a result, a new problem emerged: littering. Since bottles had become increasingly important as advertising tools, much litter was immediately visible as belonging to a particular brand (few faced this problem as directly as Coca-Cola, whose iconic bottles were designed to be recognized even in the dark).[8] As a result, the bottlers had to disown the bottles, both materially and culturally. Producers claimed that it was not their fault that the bottles were no longer reused; rather it was because consumers did not properly discard them.

Keep America Beautiful, which was established by a group of glass, aluminum, paper, and steel container manufacturers in 1953 to shift the burden of waste from producer to consumer, advocated this narrative.[9] Through this nonprofit public-education organization, beverage bottlers came out in favor of recycling. They also argued, however, that the responsibility for recycling rested with the consumers, not the producers of packaging, as demonstrated by the famous Keep America Beautiful slogan "People Start Pollution. People Can Stop It." To them, the solution to the environmental problems caused by packaging would not be solved through mandatory recycling, taxes, or deposits. As Ginger Strand writes, they wanted to focus public attention on the symptoms rather than the system.[10] Many have seen "The Crying Indian" public service announcement, hailed as a galvanizing moment in the American environmental movement.[11] In the video, released on Earth Day in 1971, a Native American (played by Italian-American actor Iron Eyes Cody) narratively represented harmony with nature and careful use of resources and faced the litter generated by American consumer society with a tear running down his cheek. Through awareness campaigns and national cleanup days, Keep America Beautiful, with the help of the Ad Council, which made the video, aimed to change consumer attitudes to littering and raise their environmental awareness. Bart Elmore argues that the Crying Indian campaign emerged as a united response from the American beverage industry to a political challenge in 1967, when no less than twenty-one states proposed a ban on one-way containers.[12]

Meanwhile, in Norway, disposable bottles were briefly introduced by some bottlers in the mid-1960s, but were rejected by the industry as a whole.[13] Their reasons did not have anything to do with environmentalism—by shutting out containers that were incompatible with their existing and costly infrastructure, it became much harder for newcomers to establish themselves in Norway. It was a way of limiting competition and protecting Norwegian workplaces that were under threat after Norway had joined EFTA, the European Free Trade Agreement, in 1960, which opened up the Norwegian market to international companies.

Some consumers were also resistant to throw away bottles, although not uniformly. While in the United States, "No deposit, no return" bottles were marketed as the pinnacle of convenience, Norwegian consumers were initially frustrated by them. What were they to do with them if they couldn't return them to the store? It could be hard to find a trash can when you were out on the move, and besides it felt wrong to not take it back to the store. This is not to say that Norwegians didn't embrace consumerism from the 1960s onward—Norway has taken part in astounding growth in both wealth and consumption, especially after finding oil in the North Sea in 1969, and this definitely influenced consumer motivations—but there were still reservations about one-way bottles as a breach of a social and economic contract.

The strongest challenge to the new disposable containers came from the political side. In Norway and Sweden, as well as many other countries, the governments have used tax incentives to motivate bottlers to either keep reusable bottles or design new return systems that ensure high recycling rates. Norway introduced a bottle bill in 1970. The same thing happened in many places in the United States. Despite the strong industry resistance that Keep America Beautiful represented, several states passed so-called bottle bills in the 1970s and 1980s. Oregon, Vermont, Michigan, Maine, Iowa, Connecticut, Delaware, New York, Massachusetts, and finally California—one by one the states passed laws requiring deposits on certain types of containers.

The relationship between bottlers and bottle bill proponents in the United States has been quite antagonistic. In Scandinavia, by contrast, this relationship was historically remarkably cooperative. While economical concerns certainly influence the logic of recycling, it is not solely based on the whims of the free market—the beverage container recycling system is maintained through direct political intervention.

As the beverage container selection has grown, recycling systems have gotten rather confusing. There is no longer such a thing as a standard, reusable bottle. In many European countries and some US state jurisdictions, containers that carry a deposit will be clearly identified with the deposit amount (the Swedish symbol even has a simplified version of the recycling arrows). Deposit-refund systems are utterly dependent on context, involving material affordances, market economies, technological developments, business strategies, political frameworks, and of course also the environmental awareness of consumers. There is a large number of actors involved in the development and maintenance of such systems, and they are motivated by more than just environmental concerns.

Beverage container recycling illustrates well how environmental concerns have shifted over time. When beverage containers first became considered an environmental problem in the 1950s and 1960s, it grew out of locally centered concerns about littering and visual pollution. Broken glass bottles were eyesores and potentially also dangerous. Today, these concerns are still alive, but another layer of more abstract concerns has joined them, centered on global issues such as resources, climate change, and environmental justice. There is no longer a black-and-white story of bottle recycling.

As with so much other waste management, the handling of materials brings with it particular ideas of class and status. One might argue that if recycling a particular material is so commonplace that everyone does it, the act of recycling does not carry a particular stigma.

For instance, in Scandinavia, the beverage container recycling infrastructure is thoroughly integrated in everyday life. Families bring their bottles back to the grocery store when they go shopping, where so-called reverse vending machines—think of it as a hole in the wall—will take their bottles and print a deposit receipt. Here, middle-class families will meet the rich, they will meet students who are bringing in the bottles after last weekend's big party, and they will meet poor people who have collected bottles from public trash cans. Everyone returns bottles in Norway.

This is not the case everywhere, however. In the United States, bottle collection and recycling has largely become associated with poverty rather than what can be considered an act of citizenship. Many American consumers leave their bottles on the curbside to be picked up by scavengers. In a way, the ragpicker we encountered in the previous chapter lives on in this role. When bottles are removed from the household sphere, a cultural transformation takes place. They become waste, and the people who collect them are influenced by it. This is the case with waste laborers across the world, whether we call then scavengers, ragpickers, or sandmen. As Doron and Jeffrey write in their study of waste in India, waste laborers "carry a burden of poverty and prejudice."[14] And they are rarely as mobile as the waste they are collecting. While their waste, through recycling, moves up the value chain, laborers tend to stay at the bottom. "Economies of recycling, as they now operate, reproduce social and economic inequalities," writes Doron and Jeffrey.[15]

We see these themes in *Redemption*, a short documentary from 2013 that earned an Academy Award nomination.[16] This film follows the life of "canners" on the streets of New York—the many poor who collect empty bottles and cans for survival. The writer Nicola Twilley suggests that in New York, the state has used bottle bills to outsource its "acts of environmental virtue, at far below minimum wage."[17] We can also interpret bottle bills—as practiced in the United States—as a system where environmental legislation needs to manage not only the environmental cost, but also the social cost of an economic system that is more concerned with profit than with people. One-sided consumer-centered recycling initiatives are a clear example of modifying the (economic) costs of particular solutions by externalizing particular costs, shifting the burden of cleaning up wastes from the producer to individuals and to the government. It is a particular kind of resource colonialism, to which we will return at the end of the book.

Bottles show how materials have affordances, to use a term from design scholar Donald Norman.[18] Their material characteristics enable certain possibilities for use,

When bottles are removed from the household sphere, a cultural transformation takes place. They become waste, and the people who collect them are influenced by the waste.

and limit others. Such affordances follow materials into their afterlives as potential waste. In the case of glass bottles, the affordance in use can be durability, but thick glass is typically required if the bottle is to be reusable, which brings with it the limitation of weight. Another affordance is transparency, which allows the contents to be seen, although in some cases, the contents can change flavor when exposed to light (which is why beer bottles are typically brown, to filter the light). But in the afterlife, the affordances of glass bottles are more closely tied to economic models based on glass and recycling incentives. Here, they enter a global marketplace where prices fluctuate.

Bottles are not simply vessels for beverages we wish to consume—they also carry and give shape to whole discourses about meaning, value, and politics.

ALUMINUM SYSTEMS AND ENERGY

There is no other metal on the earth which is so widely scattered and occurs in such abundance.

Joseph William Richards, *Aluminium: Its History, Occurrence, Properties, Metallurgy and Applications, Including Its Alloys*, 1887

Waste is unruly and hard to pin down. In part this is because waste moves around and because many actors in the waste management system seeks to keep waste outside of external control, as we have seen. It is also because waste must always be understood as bigger than a single piece of trash. An empty aluminum can never comes alone—it is merely one of billions produced and discarded every year. Conversely, there is never a single consumer recycling action—there are billions. But what do these add up to, and how? If our actions as consumers have an ecological footprint, and recycling is intended to reduce that footprint, how do we really calculate this? Where do we begin and where do we stop when we try to evaluate the environmental impact of anything?

This chapter explores how waste should primarily be understood, not as an individual problem, but rather as an infrastructural problem. While many premodern forms of recycling largely took place within households or limited geographical areas, one of the things that characterizes much modern recycling is that it takes place in large socio-technical systems. We will use aluminum as our entrance to this discussion, in part because this material intersects with both consumer and industrial systems.

How can we understand a system? "The system must be first," wrote pioneering historian of technology Thomas P. Hughes in his magisterial work *American Genesis*. "To associate modern technology solely with individual machines and devices is to overlook deeper currents of modern technology ... in highly organized and controlled technological systems."[1] Technological systems tend to move from open to closed in that the systems builders seek to bring things in under their control as a way of reducing uncertainty.[2] This can involve control over input (resources) and control over output (markets). In the modern world, recycling must be seen through a systems lens. The movements of matter and waste take place in infrastructure systems. Examples of systems are water, gas, electricity, the postal service, roads—what are sometimes called public services.

Waste must always be understood as bigger than a single piece of trash.

In these systems, private and public sectors meet. In her study of "garbage citizenship" in Senegal, Rosalind Fredericks argues that infrastructures are "ecologies that assemble a range of spatialized relationships between political economic imperatives, technologies, natural processes, forms of sociality, social meanings, and modes of ritual action."[3] Infrastructures actively shape the world around us, "not simply in the materials and energies it avails, but also the way it attracts people, draws them in, coalesces and expends their capacities."[4]

An infrastructural approach allows us to consider the environmental impact of recycling. In theory, this would let us decide which materials are most environmentally friendly for a given usage and which actions and incentives are the best for making people recycle. Only then can we say whether recycling actually matters. But defining the boundaries of a given infrastructural system is not a straightforward task. Evaluating the success of recycling systems brings its own challenges. For instance, at what point of a product's life can and should its environmental impact be measured? How far upstream and downstream of the product's period of active use should we go? How many factors are relevant and practical to include in accounting for environmental impact? These are questions that are easy—and relevant—to ask, but fully answering them is more difficult than one might think.

Aluminum cans provide us with a good case for studying how the definition of what is in and out of the system affects whether the material can be considered environmentally friendly. Aluminum was once a precious metal, even more so than gold and silver. While aluminum is the most common metal on earth, it required significant improvements in production before the material was sufficiently affordable that it could become a critical part of modern society. Creating aluminum takes several steps. First, raw bauxite ore is crushed and processed through the Bayer process to create aluminum oxide. Then this aluminum oxide can be smelted using the Hall-Héroult process to create pure aluminum. Both these processes were invented in the late 1800s and were fundamental to the mass production of aluminum. The result was a complex and energy-intensive process that creates a considerable amount of waste byproducts—bauxite tailings often called "red mud," classified as a hazardous material that currently has few uses. Today, aluminum is generally produced where energy is plentiful and affordable, which means that the raw material bauxite is shipped to the place of processing.[5] Aluminum is an essential part of the manufactured world—it is used in infrastructure, cars, airplanes, construction, and packaging, among other things. The material history of aluminum closely follows that of glass bottles, of dramatically reduced prices and increased availability over time.

Aluminum is one of the most recyclable materials we have. The energy cost of producing virgin aluminum is high, but the material can be nearly endlessly melted down and recycled without any loss of quality for only 5 percent of the energy cost. In this sense, it differs considerably from paper, which constantly degrades through recycling. Aluminum also has other material qualities that make it attractive for a wide range of applications. This is especially true of aluminum beverage containers, as the material is light and durable, does not let light into the container, and does not impart any flavor on the contents. It also carried an aura of modernity and progress that many older materials did not.[6]

Aluminum cans replaced steel cans in the late 1960s. These were lighter and meant lower transportation costs for the beverage companies. Aluminum beverage cans are now the most-recycled consumer product in the United States, yet this is because of the great quantity of cans produced, not because the return rate has increased; as Elizabeth Royte writes, "their rate of return fell from a peak of 65 percent in 1992 to a twenty-three-year low of 44 percent in 2003, when 820,000 tons of aluminum cans were trashed."[7] According to estimates from the Container Recycling Institute, more than a trillion aluminum cans have been thrown away and buried in landfills, recyclable but unrecycled, since 1972. Such high numbers have become so abstract that it is hard to make sense of them. Again according to Royte, "the amount is nearly equal in weight to the world's entire annual output of primary aluminum ingot." This tells us something about the vast amount of aluminum cans in use—they cannot be meaningfully considered as individual objects managed by individual consumer actions.

Despite this, aluminum is a poster child for recycling, since it doesn't degrade and the value remains high. Many consumer products contain aluminum that can be recycled—not just the beverage can, but also aluminum foil, computers, telephones, bicycles, ladders, furniture, and cookware. Add to this the vast mass of industrial uses, such as airplanes, cars, trains, bridges, and buildings. After the aluminum product is collected for recycling, it gets taken to a treatment plant for cleaning and melting into ingots that can be used for making new products. Such processing requires only 5 percent of the energy needed for virgin aluminum production. For producers using aluminum in their products, turning to recycled scrap aluminum makes perfect sense.[8] Companies like Alcoa, Pepsi, Coca-Cola, and Boeing all use massive amounts of scrap aluminum in their products, so they have motivation for promoting recycling of this material.

In 2017, about 27 percent of the total American aluminum production came from recycled discarded aluminum products. More than half of this recycled aluminum comes from beer and soft drink cans. One consequence is that the model for recycling these cans comes from older systems established to manage glass bottles, where legislation provides the incentive that purely economic approaches cannot, as we saw in the previous chapter.

In aluminum's movements from raw material to manufactured object and back again, the material moves in time and space, coming into contact with many actors, discourses, and different recycling processes. An object—any object—puts its imprint on the world in a variety of ways, and finding the boundaries of that imprint is not an easy matter. We have already talked about the idea of a waste stream, and now we will add two more words to our vocabulary: upstream and downstream. Any manufactured object has an environmental impact upstream—in the extraction of raw materials and in the production of the object; and downstream, in the discarding and disposal of the object. Including upstream and downstream perspectives is a recognition that objects exist in time as well as space, and that they affect the environment in different ways throughout their whole lifecycles—and afterlives. Technological systems encompass both the upstream and downstream of a product's life, but the boundaries of such systems can be manipulated for different purposes.

The environmental impact of aluminum can change considerably the further upstream one goes. We briefly discussed bauxite mining and the generation of "red mud" hazardous waste. Bauxite is typically found close to the

In aluminum's movements from raw material to manufactured object and back again, the material moves in time and space, coming into contact with many actors, discourses, and different recycling processes.

surface, so strip mines are the most common form of mines used. This creates huge landscape scars, leads to deforestation, and destroys wildlife habitats.[9] Bauxite mines can be found across the world, but the largest producers are Australia, China, Russia, Canada, and India. The high energy demands of processing the bauxite into aluminum means that the bauxite generally must be transported to places with high energy production, typically hydropower, and these places are not always close to the place of extraction. This transport generates emissions. The energy consumed in processing also comes with environmental costs, whether it is based on coal, nuclear energy, or hydropower. China is the largest producer of aluminum in the world, and the massive energy requirements have been one of the drivers for China's many dam projects. Each of these has long-reaching environmental consequences.

In trying to assess the environmental impact of aluminum recycling, it becomes clear how everything is connected to everything else, in a complex web of relations. Trying to isolate the impact of any single thing on this web triggers cascading effects, like ripples on water. One object can be more resource demanding in its production, but has a longer lifespan than other products. Some might require much energy in use, but are easier to dispose of responsibly than others. Some are expensive in use, but have low environmental impact in use, raising the issue of how you convert between different types of costs and value. Not that this stops people from trying, and in practice it is a question of how far out you want to set the boundaries of your impact assessment, and which factors you consider relevant for the equation. The further out, the more representative of the actual world the assessment ends up, but the complexity also increases exponentially.

The scientific method for measuring such environmental costs is called life cycle analysis (LCA).[10] One of the first attempts at developing such analyses was an (unpublished) study that quantified the "resource requirements, emission loadings, and waste flows of different beverage containers," conducted by Midwest Research Institute (MRI) for the Coca-Cola Company in 1969.[11] Here, Bart Elmore writes, the MRI "looked at various types of throwaway containers, and compared them with returnable glass bottles on almost every measure: energy expenditure, waste generation, water pollution, air emissions and more." The conclusion was that, based on these criteria, throwaway containers could not match the environmental efficiency of returnable glass bottles that were reused an average of ten times.[12]

The approaches that the MRI pioneered in their study became highly influential on the way industry ended up measuring the environmental impact of their products and activities. Tim Cooper writes how LCA has "has helped government and industry to determine appropriate standards (e.g., for eco-labeling), make product comparisons, verify environmental claims, and assess policy options," despite being "highly complex and fraught with difficulties concerning methodology and data collection."[13] By considering the whole life spans of products, in what is sometimes called "cradle to grave" or "womb to tomb" approaches, the system character becomes evident. It is not meaningful to measure the impact of any single object at one specific point in time, such as at the time of production, time of purchase, or time of disposal. LCA has developed since then to be a method with broad applicability, but beverage container recycling debates have frequently returned to it.

In Norway, the introduction of aluminum cans was tied to the introduction of a new deposit system where taxes on disposable containers were tied to their actual recycling rate. The Resirk system, as it was called, depended heavily on the use of LCA models and arguments in the extended and often heated debates over the relative qualities of different types of materials. This debate demonstrates the difficulty of providing objective answers to the question of a product's environmental cost. In the Resirk debates, life-cycle analyses and other methods from industrial ecology, to which we will return in chapter 9, became a battleground for both sides of the debate. The results derived from these methods equally supported both standpoints, all depending on what they chose to include as relevant factors and where they set the boundaries for their systems. The ways in which these questions were framed helped establish the "greenness" of disposable aluminum containers as a boundary object that both sides could engage each other around, all while more or less circumventing and under-communicating a number of other agendas related to labor interests and trade protection.[14]

Competing LCA analyses of the same object do not necessarily come to the same conclusions, which has led to considerable criticism of the method. While some point to errors in setting system boundaries as a main cause of such differing results, others argue that there are in fact no agreed-upon standards for how to set boundaries and how to decide which factors to include.[15] LCA can never include *all* relevant factors, owing to the simple fact that it is impossible to fully capture the complexity of the world in models. This opens up for selection and potential manipulation of results. In Dietmar Offenhuber's study of waste and information, he explores exactly this issue.[16] The lack of information and transparency on what happens with waste globally makes it difficult to evaluate. Unruly waste evades control. The lesson here is that the actual benefit of recycling depends on a whole range of factors, many of which it is not possible to get reliable data.

Many other factors are not as much related to the material itself, but with the actual movement of the material across the planet. Offenhuber studies how transportation plays a key role in the actual environmental impact of recycling and how LCA models attempt to track this. For instance, an LCA approach called WARM (waste reduction model) calculates the emission of greenhouse gases for transportation of different types of materials, based on their weight and mass. This model shows that materials such as paper, cardboard, and metal have high greenhouse gas savings when recycled with state-of-the-art processes. The actual savings with plastics varies wildly because of the many different types of plastics in use (which we will return to in the next chapter). Savings with glass are also not easy to calculate.[17]

Considering products and materials as part of larger systems—or indeed as part of society, with all the culture and politics that follows—complicates the situation for those who want absolute answers, but it also provides opportunities for deliberate interventions in the way we make, use, and discard things. While product designers, the ones who give shape to many of the things that make up the material world, can rightly be criticized for not having considered or minimized the environmental cost of their products, there has been a significant shift in recent years, where an increasing number of designers have reconsidered their social and environmental responsibility.

Design can be seen as both a matter of ideology and a matter of materiality. In the first case, design can influence people to act and think in particular ways. In the second case, design has material and environmental consequences both upstream and downstream of the actual designed object. For instance, designers can choose to use different materials with lower environmental costs or different social justice implications, to strip down products to use less materials, to pick more recyclable materials, and so on.[18]

Yet we are still faced with the question of necessity—do we really need to make all these things? The disposable aluminum coffee pod illustrates this point well. Pioneered as the Keurig K-Cup, the coffee pod allowed consumers to conveniently make single cups of coffee in specialized coffee makers. Keurig's containers are made from plastic, with paper and metal components. Keurig argues that their K-Cups are fully recyclable, although the individual components of the K-Cup have to be separated for this to be true. One of Keurig's main competitors, Nespresso, uses aluminum capsules instead. In 2012, Nespresso sold more than 27 billion such capsules.[19] These are in theory recyclable, but without extensive recycling systems in place, they are likely to be discarded on the altar of consumer convenience. Design incorporates far more than just individual products, as these must always be considered as part of larger social and technological infrastructures. Design can serve to make processes both upstream and downstream visible to consumers—but it can also obscure them.[20] Nespresso has implemented its own recycling program where capsules can be returned to their stores, but the company will not disclose how many capsules are actually recycled.

Debbie Chakra has argued that technological systems are "one of the main ways that we take care of each other at scale."[21] She was focusing on the role of technology in society and how it could be used to improve democracy, but the same can be said about waste. In both cases, technological systems need to be made "more visible, understandable, and valued by the general public." Waste is unruly, but systems allow us to exert an influence on it.

Design can serve
to make processes
both upstream and
downstream visible to
consumers—but it can
also obscure them.

PLASTIC FUTURES

Mr. McGuire: I want to say one word to you. Just one word.

Benjamin: Yes, sir.

Mr. McGuire: Are you listening?

Benjamin: Yes, I am.

Mr. McGuire: Plastics.

Benjamin: Exactly how do you mean?

Mr. McGuire: There's a great future in plastics. Think about it. Will you think about it?

The Graduate, 1967

Plastic was once touted as the material of the future. It has been associated with newness. Yet, plastic rapidly lost its luster. Today, plastic is everywhere, but it is generally seen as a low-value material—fake, cheap, ersatz. The question of plastics recycling brings us into an even messier territory than glass, paper, and aluminum do. Plastic comes in many varieties, which generally require different recycling processes. Plastic also degrades with recycling, meaning that unlike aluminum, plastic at some point inevitably turns to waste, material without value.

Plastic didn't even exist 150 years ago. While quasi-plastic materials such as celluloid and shellac were in use for consumer and industrial products earlier, Leo Baekeland's 1907 invention, Bakelite, was the first fully synthetic plastic. Since then, we have had a proliferation of plastic materials. Most plastics are used for industrial purposes where consumers never have an option to recycle it. This matters for how we approach plastics waste. Environmental campaigns often target consumer plastic such as plastic straws and plastic bags, but most is used behind the scenes, in construction and in supply chains.

The challenge with plastics recycling is that technically, there is no such thing as plastic. There are instead many different plastics, each with different material qualities. Technically, plastics are synthetic or partially synthetic polymers, usually derived from petrochemicals, although some bioplastics are made with other organic materials. Each type of plastic requires different processing for recycling. Experts can tell different plastics apart by look

The challenge with plastics recycling is that technically, there is no such thing as plastic. There are instead many different plastics, each with different material qualities.

and feel—for instance, Doron and Jeffrey describe how Indian waste sorters have developed the necessary know-how. Most people—assuming they even care—have to depend on the packaging labeling, a recycling arrow triangle with a number in the center (see box).[1] This type of labeling matters. Offenhuber argues that this is a matter of information and transparency: with recycling, the devil is in the details, and getting to those details can be difficult.[2]

Plastic was understood in the mid-twentieth century as a miracle material: cheap, durable, and infinitely malleable. In the 1940s and 1950s, plastic signaled prosperity and progress.[3] Historian Ylva Sjöstrand demonstrates how after plastic broke through in Sweden in 1950, the weight of plastic in the waste stream increased exponentially. The expanding amount of plastic into the waste stream caused problems with incineration, which at the time was a common strategy for dealing with waste: while plastic would burn, PVC made hydrochloric acid during incineration, which would cause damage to the bricks in the smokestacks. The incinerator in Högdalen had long periods of interruptions and rebuilding during its first years in operation thanks to this.[4] Landfilling plastic was also a problem, as plastics would never decompose.

Whatever its environmental costs may be, plastic is a material that has replaced many older materials. In the case of beverage containers, while glass and aluminum

**How to identify plastics by the number inside
the recycling triangle**

1. PET (polyethylene terephthalate) is the most
commonly recycled plastic, often used in bottles.

2. HDPE (high-density polyethylene) is used
for packaging, in particular food, as it does not
transmit chemicals into the contents.

3. PVC (polyvinyl chloride) is very resistant to
chemicals and bacteria, so it is used for medical
purposes, but also in flooring, pipes, shower
curtains, and car dashboards

4. LDPE (low-density polyethylene) is durable
and flexible, often used for plastic bags,
wrapping, and wires. It is not commonly recycled.

5. PP (polypropylene) is temperature resistant
and is often used for packaging that will be
heated or cooled.

6. PS (polystyrene or Styrofoam) is used for
packaging and disposables such as cups and trays.

7. The big "other" category, with many different
plastics that are hard to recycle.

cans still exist, plastic has taken over. PET plastic bottles are highly functional objects for bottlers. They are light, durable, and nonbreakable, and they show off their content in ways that can be used for marketing and branding. They don't break like glass. Another common selling point is that the PET plastic used in beverage plastic bottles is inert and does not influence the content—it does not contain any of the BPA, phthalates, dioxins, lead, cadmium, or endocrine disruptors that have become the problem with many other plastics. However, this claim has been criticized by others who point to findings of unexpected substances in bottled water. The origin of these substances has not yet been clearly identified.[5]

PET bottles were invented by DuPont engineer Nathaniel Wyeth in 1973.[6] Since their use became widespread in the 1980s, they have become ubiquitous. Philosopher Gay Hawkins has made the case that PET bottles are "made to be wasted."[7] She criticizes many standard histories of the plastics industry for sometimes rendering plastic "a passive object of economic forces."[8] With this she means that the disposability of PET bottles is a matter of design; the qualities of the bottle are not intrinsic, but have to be produced. As a result, plastic bottles must be considered as part of the larger systems they move through.

As Bart Elmore has documented, Coca-Cola moved toward plastic bottles because the company "believed recycling systems would allow the company to reclaim much of the plastic it used."[9] Coca-Cola began shifting to plastic containers in the late 1960s, and fully committed to it in the mid-1970s.[10] The LCA analysis MRI did was motivated by this move. Coca-Cola first attempted to use Lopac bottles, a type of plastic, but these were banned by the FDA for being carcinogenic. When Coca-Cola and Pepsi switched to plastic PET bottles in the late 1970s, they had greater success and plastic bottles started filling up waste sites and landfills.

Instead of the old deposit systems, beverage manufacturers were in favor of curbside recycling programs, where consumers could leave their recyclables outside their house for pickup. Curbside recycling is a mostly American system, and it arose out of a particular historical context. Such programs grew rapidly in the United States, writes Elmore, leading many industries to abandon their own buy-back programs in favor of municipal services that cost them nothing.[11] By the 1980s, most places in the United States had ended up with curbside recycling programs. Corporations saw these as a way to avoid extended producer responsibility. The belief in the high material value of beverage containers helped fund the whole program, yet it was really only scrap aluminum that had high market value. As an environmental measure, they are a complete failure compared with the systems they replaced. Elmore does not mince words: "American citizens traditionally averse to corporate welfare were essentially bailing out industries that remained largely exempt from disposal fees, but they continued to do so in part because the decentralized funding structure of recycling kept the collective costs of the system hidden."[12] Samantha Mac-Bride, who wrote the leading study of recycling, shares this critique of curbside recycling systems: since they offer no financial incentives to recycle, 70 percent of plastic containers are never recycled.[13]

This development was not universal, however. PET bottles have followed different trajectories across the world. When PET bottles came to Germany, they entered a market with existing recycling systems. Andrea Westermann describes how it wasn't until the late 1980s that West Germany managed to implement a PET bottle recycling system. The final push that got the system implemented was the considerable importing of beverages in nonreturnable vinyl bottles from other European countries. As would be the case in Scandinavia later, the German state insisted that PET bottles could be accepted only as part of functioning recycling systems. Coca-Cola and other beverage producers took the challenge to make systems modeled on the older glass bottle recycling systems.[14]

In Norway, PET bottles followed yet another trajectory. Faced with extensive debates about how bad disposable containers were in comparison to the reusable glass bottle, the food and beverage company Nora came up with the idea of a reusable PET bottle in the mid-1980s. Made out of much thicker plastic than the disposable bottles, these bottles could be reused up to twenty-five times. Compared to glass, these thick plastic bottles were still lighter, which made transportation more affordable; very durable, which made breakages rare; and quieter, which made bottling facilities a better place to work. Such bottles were easily integrated into existing deposit-refund infrastructures, as they did not challenge the underlying premise of reusable bottles.[15] Over time, however, one-way disposable plastic bottles have become more and more common in Norway.

Single-use PET bottles may be technically recyclable, but they are often not recycled. Tony Clarke's exposé of the bottled water industry demonstrates that only a small percentage of bottles make it into effective recycling facilities."[16] Another recent study argued that as little as only 9 percent of all plastic had been recycled. Twelve percent had been incinerated, and the rest has ended up in landfills or in the natural environment.[17]

The thin PET bottles that are so ubiquitous today are problematic even when collected, since there are limited uses for them. Close cooperation on the industrial design side could hold one potential key to improvement, in designing products from the recycled material. My office chair, made by the company HÅG, uses some material from recycled PET bottles. Fleece fabric and other textiles can also have fibers from recycled PET bottles. For instance,

Patagonia uses PET bottle fibers in their fleece clothing. Making recycled PET bottles—so-called "rPET"—is also possible, but these do not look as transparent and shiny as fresh plastic. There have been attempts at making alternative plastics for bottles, such as cornstarch plastic (PLA). But within this recycling system this is problematic because PLA plastic contaminates PET plastic, which makes recycling even more challenging.

The plastic bottle symbolizes the main issue with recycling. On its own, it is insignificant. In the billions, it does matter. A million plastic bottles are bought every minute around the world. There is massive growth in China, as bottled beverages come into economic reach of more people. China does not have official recycling programs (at least not in any major cities), but an army of informal trash collectors keep most bottles out of landfills. China is turning toward a throwaway culture; throwing away packaging is seen as wealth.

We can take bottled water as a reminder that not all forms of disposables are wholly bad. In some places there are good reasons to drink bottled water, such as Flint, Michigan, which has not had safe drinking water since 2014. But bottled water also represents a technological fix: instead of repairing (communal, shared) infrastructure that can provide safe and good drinking water from the tap, we can just use (individualized) solutions such as bottles, provided by the private sector. Should one instead

The plastic bottle symbolizes the main issue with recycling. On its own, it is insignificant. In the billions, it does matter.

invest in better water infrastructure? As with recycling, a single consumer can't fix the larger underlying problem alone. But he or she can get clean water by drinking bottled water. The sociologist Andrew Szasz introduced the concept of "inverse quarantine" to characterize the way in which many consumers seek to protect themselves from the uncertainty of environmental problems through individual solutions. While mobility has been a significant driver behind the popularity of bottled water, the fear of contamination is also a significant factor. Consumerism brought us from protecting the environment to protecting ourselves.[18] Recycling has the potential to be an act of citizenship, of participating in a larger society with rights and responsibility. But it can also be seen as an individual act of seeking redemption. The sense of environmental security bottled waters offers is usually not false, but there are also costs.

While we have known about the environmental challenges of plastic in a wide range of places for decades, the oceans have served as a particularly critical site for engaging with plastic waste in recent years. Long considered a virtually bottomless sink in which trash could be dumped, the oceans suddenly have gotten much smaller and have been thoroughly changed by human activities. On their way to the ocean, rivers pick up waste from the entirety of human civilization. Plastic is a not insignificant part of this waste, ranging from large objects to microplastics.

Waste covers the surface of the ocean, as for instance in the so-called Great Pacific Garbage Patch, but has also reached the very deepest points of the planet. A recent study found a disposable plastic bag at the bottom of the Mariana Trench, 36,000 feet under the surface.[19] Over time, plastic also breaks into ever-smaller pieces. This microplastic evades the attempted ocean cleanup operations. Plastic doesn't go away. Instead, we end up with new geological terms such as plastiglomerates, coined by Patricia Corcoran, an expert in sedimentary petrology, who studied the amalgams of plastic, volcanic rock, seashells, and corals found on the beaches of Hawaii. As Amanda Boetzkes writes, "the plastiglomerate is a symptom of the Anthropocene."[20]

Both the sheer mass of visible plastic and the invisible pervasiveness of microplastics have upended previous ideas of boundaries between the natural and cultural, the pure and the polluted. One example is the dead goose-beaked whale found on the west coast of Norway in 2017. Upon examining it, scientists found 30 plastic bags and smaller pieces of plastic in its stomach.[21] The powerful images taken by photographer Chris Jordan of dead albatrosses with plastic in their stomachs, surrounded by plastic debris at Midway Island, are also poignant and uncomfortable. These islands are thousands of miles away from the nearest inhabited place, yet the plastic waste of modern consumer society has penetrated and damaged local ecosystems. If we are to believe the latest microplastic pollution studies, the same is really the case in our bodies, which are becoming infiltrated by plastics. Plastics and the chemicals they so often contain make the boundaries between our bodies and the rest of the world uncertain. Environmental historian Nancy Langston has demonstrated how endocrine disruptors often used in plastics of different types has led to significant human harm and has leached out into the environment.[22]

The oceans are full of waste, but where does it come from? A mapping of coastal trash in Norway estimates that most of the trash in Northern waters likely stems from the fisheries industry—and most of it plastic.[23] Globally, other estimates indicate that such "ghost" fishing equipment that has been lost or discarded at sea comprises up to 10 percent of all marine litter.[24] In doing these surveys, the research team from the Norwegian Marine Research Institute (Havforskningsinstituttet) found plastics and other trash much further out than they expected. In places they found up to seven tons of plastic per square kilometer. This survey did not include microplastics. The marine plastics waste is a serious concern to the Norwegian marine industries, which has founded a Marine Recycling Network. This network aims to map, research, collect, and process ocean waste. It remains to be seen if this initiative will have any significant impact.

And they are not alone in trying to deal with ocean plastic waste. The last few years, the nonprofit organization Ocean Cleanup has received significant media attention. Founded by the young Dutch inventor Boyan Slat, the organization aims to create passive drifting systems that will follow the ocean currents to sift floating waste out of the water. At some point after capture, the accumulated plastic will be collected and taken to land. What happens later with this collected waste is uncertain. Their goal of cleaning up the oceans is well intended, but many have questioned if this will have any impact. The organization states that there are more than five trillion pieces of plastic littering the ocean, most of it accumulating in five ocean garbage patches created by currents. Numerically breaking down the waste problem in this way makes it sound manageable, but as we have seen throughout this book, waste evades such control.

"Material specificity matters for action," argues Max Liboiron.[25] "Without paying close attention to the ways materials are located within wider material and social systems, solutions to their presence are often stillborn." She is particularly critiquing the ocean cleanup plans that assume that marine microplastics are larger than five millimeters. Nor do they consider the sheer size of the oceans. Ocean cleanups will never be more than—literally and metaphorically—a drop in the ocean. Liboiron actively speaks out against the small steps consumers can take to reduce their ecological footprint through recycling, as these have very little impact on the large majority of plastic waste.[26] Instead, we need to move upstream to the sites of production.

Writer and sociologist Rebecca Altman reminds us, through her article on the plastic grocery bag, that disposability is designed; it is historically a new idea that had to be actively promoted.[27] Altman argues that teaching people to throw things away was "a systematic rerouting of human behavior and norms." Before plastic bags supplanted paper grocery bags, shoppers were satisfied with the functionality of paper bags. In order to promote plastic, the Plastic Grocery Sack Council started a campaign that sold plastic bags as reusable. This was true: they are, potentially, both reusable and recyclable. In our Scandinavian household, where we very rarely accept new plastic bags from stores, we reuse the bags we still have accumulated over the years all the time. This is possible because Scandinavian plastic bags are required by law to be thick and durable; they feel like premium plastic. Contrast this with American ones, which are ultralight and thin, tearing at the least tension. It is these bags that so easily are taken by the wind, flying around to end up in trees and other structures. Material choices matter.

The challenges that consumers face with plastics are considerable. Which plastic is this? What should we do with it? If I put it in the right box, what happens with it then? Such concerns appeared on the radar as early as the 1970s, when plastics became redefined as an environmental hazard—initially tied to the growing amounts of plastic waste.[28] In this process, consumers all over Europe built on traditional practices of collecting and reusing materials, while at the same time shifting their reasons for doing so, as historians Ruth Oldenziel and Heike Weber argue.[29] It was during this period that recycling became an ecological duty rather than a way of coping with scarcity. Historian Andrea Westermann demonstrates how consumers trying to make decisions about plastics use and recycling "consistently emphasised the difficulty of getting the product information they needed to make an informed choice in the market place."[30] This is not just the case with plastics, of course, but with any environmentalist action. How do we know that the things we choose to (or are forced to) do actually matter? How do we know that the outcomes of our actions end up aligning with our intentions? Here we come back to Offenhuber's information point: knowing what happens with waste is a concern not just in environmental governance, but also for consumers.

Plastic was the future. But is it still the future? The material choices we make as a society entail long-term responsibilities. Recycling can be good, but reuse or reduction is generally better. Recycling is after-the-fact clean up, and there might not be anything worthwhile to do with the recycled material. Recycling is a last resort.

Plastics exist in deep time. They come from dinosaurs and plant matter from eons past. They will live long after us. However, plastics do not stay pristine and untouched. The malleability that made the product so useful to its many users also leads to the difficulties of properly classifying, sorting, and returning discarded materials to production. The various polymers called plastics are often integrated into designs where they become hybridized or, in the words of Paola Antonelli, "mutant materials," that take on new characteristics and fill new roles.[31] This is also true for their afterlife. They degrade yet they don't disappear. Some waste is forever—there is no away for it to go to. No longer the material of tomorrow, it is the waste of forever. While we can endlessly discuss the best ways of collecting plastic waste for recycling, there is no final solution. There is no putting plastic back in its Pandora's box.

MINING E-WASTE

"Away" is a place.

Ebenezer Furkuo Amankwaa et al.[1]

Throughout 2017, millions of Norwegian radios (some estimate up to twenty million) went obsolete more or less overnight, when the government switched off the national FM broadcast band in stages, in favor of digital DAB+ radio. The intentions behind shifting to digital radio were good, as the new standard could provide national network access for twenty-five, rather than only five, channels. Audio quality was higher and the transmission could also include text and data information, which consumers had grown to expect from other forms of digital media. The only downside was that existing FM radios (as well as the estimated quarter-million radios using the older DAB standard) were unable to access the new digital radio signals. As the analog radio band grew silent, the sheer material mass of millions now-obsolete radios loomed. What to do with them all?

One could simply buy a new radio, of course, and not worry about the rest. But Norwegians generally don't have only one radio—they have several spread throughout the house, more at the cabin, plus one in each car. All these radios add up. Many old radios could be upgraded through an external digital radio dongle—in effect, using the old radio as a speaker. Some proposed shipping the radios to places where they could be reused. After all, Norway is the only country in the world that had gone to the dramatic step of switching off the FM band. The Norwegian Missionary Society collected radios to send to Cameroon, where they would distribute them for free to people who wanted to listen to Christian radio stations. Some municipal waste management companies started collecting radios in order to send functioning radios to other European and African countries.

Many consumers did not take this well and wrote outraged letters to newspapers in 2017, pointing out the environmental waste of scrapping so many radios (although typically after complaining about the cost of upgrading). It turned out that environmental consequences were not at all on the agenda when the Norwegian Storting decided to turn off the FM band. Newspapers and consumer websites tried to put a positive spin on the story, alternating between highlighting the new and improved functionality of the DAB+ transmissions and stressing that far from all radios needed to be discarded, and of the ones that were, 80 to 90 percent of the material could be recycled or reused.

This Norwegian radio story is not yet over, and there have been significant demands for the reactivation of the old FM network. It turns out, however, that the old physical transmission infrastructure had already been dismantled and sold off. Reinstituting an old technological system after a new one is in place is not always easy. But the story gives us a good entrance into the world of e-waste recycling.

E-waste, waste coming from electronics, is a mess, materially. In our electronic gadgets, plastic, metal, circuit boards, wires, rare earth minerals, and gold are all squished into ever-smaller and more compact containers, often held together by glue. Most of the individual materials are technically recyclable, but practically it is highly demanding and labor intensive. What's worse, electronics become obsolete at an ever-faster rate, and we keep buying more and more of it. Some categories of electronic products are more or less necessities of participating in the modern world, such as cell phones and computers, and the vast infrastructures they require in order to function. Our lives have become literally and metaphorically entangled with electronic products and e-waste.

E-waste is currently the fastest-growing waste category in the world.[2] The generation of e-waste is so tied to

E-waste, waste coming from electronics, is a mess, materially.

global production and wealth distribution patterns that any significant mitigation strategies will have far-reaching implications. In a waste study led by sociologist Myra Hird, the conclusion was that waste is typically managed "in ways that do not disturb circuits of mass production and mass consumption."[3] In other words, "many of the measures that are currently taken to manage e-waste are system-preserving rather than system-challenging," as media scholar Jennie Olofsson and sociologist Franc Mali have argued. While we are encouraged to recycle obsolete electronic products, people are rarely encouraged to question the underlying system or production and consumption.[4] Information technology is often portrayed as belonging to a virtual world, but it has a very material side as well. There has been a wave of scholarship in recent years that explores the contrast between the immaterial digital and the actual reality of matter.[5] The way e-waste is generated and managed is a deeply political process, in other words, and the material consequences of e-waste recycling also "require work to become political issues."[6]

This is a challenge for consumers. As Elizabeth Royte writes, "the general public is at once wildly enthusiastic to 'recycle' its electronic waste and wildly ignorant about how this is done."[7] Where do your old electronics end up? How can you, assuming that you care, be certain that your old phone or TV is handled in an environmentally responsible manner? Such questions are getting more and more urgent in an age of planned obsolescence and new models every year. Constant upgrades make last year's model seem old.

Recycling obsolete consumer goods is nothing new. Roman iron from nails, hinges, gates, and windows was resmelted by people in medieval England who no longer had the skills and equipment to make new iron from ore, but who were perfectly capable of resmelting iron to make new tools. This form of recycling was driven by impoverishment and deskilling.[8] As people lost the skills and tools to extract and refine new metal, scavenging and recycling Roman buildings became the way most of the people in lowland Britain supplied themselves with metal for several hundred years.[9] But recycling this kind of material was relatively straightforward because of the simplicity of the component material.

Compared to iron nails and many other types of waste, e-waste is a very complex category, encompassing many different products such as computers, cell phones, televisions, monitors, cables, batteries, household appliances, and so on. Each of these products is in itself a complex combination of different kinds of materials, whether they are metal, plastic, or other elements. These materials can be both valuable and toxic; most often they are both, which means that the recycling of e-waste is both attractive and dangerous. As a category of waste, e-waste is a peculiar mix of abundance and scarcity. Rare earth minerals can be hard to come by and some are under tight geographic national control, which makes them prime recycling candidates. There is no one process for effectively recycling such products, nor can such processes remain unchanged for long, as ever-new products enter the waste stream. Finally, the processes of recycling e-waste can be highly polluting in and of themselves.

For these and other reasons, e-waste is even more unruly than the other waste categories we have seen. Because of the labor-intensive recycling requirements and the high environmental cost of recycling, much e-waste from industrialized countries with strict measures for what to do with e-waste has flowed globally to places with little- or not-enforced legal regulation of recycling.[10] The Basel Convention, which took effect in 1989, aims to restrict and control the movement of hazardous waste across national borders, in other words limiting the trade of e-waste.[11] Fifty-three countries have signed the convention; the United States is the only developed country that has not ratified this treaty, depending instead on a voluntary certification for meeting recycling standards. Another example is the WEEE Directive, which implements an Extended Producer Responsibility principle in the European Union members and associated states. This directive is intended to promote and enable reuse and recycling of material to reduce e-waste. Thanks to this directive, I can return any electronic product to retailers for proper disposal.

But what is proper disposal? The sheer mass of e-waste and the valuable materials that they contain have given rise to urban mining as one recycling strategy. Geographer Richard Grant writes that this "phenomenon is derived from the reality that the planetary ecosystem is finite, non-growing, and materially closed," so rather than mining virgin materials out of the earth, we can mine recyclable materials out of our own waste.[12] This does not exclusively involve e-waste; in the 1980s there were significant initiatives exploring aluminum extraction from American waste sites.[13]

In the wealthy part of the Western world, we have come to think about recycling and resource reclamation as a something that is handled by anonymous technologies, more or less automatically, as long as we as consumers manage to put it in the right bin. The journalist and author Adam Minter has explored the work required to process American recyclables shipped abroad to Asia, where much of the labor is done by manual workers.[14] When e-waste moves across the world, it will often change owners multiple times, which is one of the reasons why it is so hard to track. According to some estimates, up to 80 percent of e-waste ends up in developing countries, although Josh Lepawsky and Chris McNabb argue that this "pollution haven" hypothesis has weak support in trade transaction statistics.[15]

E-waste is a waste category that is notoriously difficult to quantify and map, according to Lepawsky.[16] In 2015, the e-Trash Transparency Project made an attempt to track American e-waste across the planet by placing small GPS trackers on printers and monitors that they delivered to Goodwill and other recyclers across the country. They found that about a third of the tracked objects ended up in countries with laws against importing e-waste, such as Hong Kong. The sample was small and there are many possible sources of error, but it illustrates well how many gaps there are in the legal frameworks targeting the trade of e-waste. Since 2008, American companies have been unable to export mercury for disposal in other countries, but there are no laws stopping the export of other toxic materials. A Seattle-based recycling company was fined $444,000 when it was caught shipping mercury-containing flat-screen televisions and monitors to Hong Kong.

When China in 2018 announced that it would no longer import e-waste, many countries had to rethink their e-waste management strategies. The whole e-waste and recycling industry had kept a close eye on developments in China, which notified the World Trade Organization in the summer of 2017 that it planned to ban imports of some types of "foreign garbage."[17] Because of the surplus of cheap labor in parts of Asia, it had been possible for scrap to get "recycled completely, providing a relatively clean alternative to mined, virgin materials," and still be profitable (which is key to making business do anything green). Minter argues that China is "desperate to show environmental leadership" and that labor conditions actually are much better than one would think.[18] China's scrap recycling industry has evolved into a "critical supplier of raw materials to respected manufacturers of iPhones, PCs, automobile engines, and other precision manufactured high-tech products." In the end, Minter turns the exploitation story on its head: "I simply can't escape the feeling that the people being exploited are the Americans sending all that value to China." Other countries such as Thailand and Vietnam are now considering following China's example, most likely as a response to increased volume of imports after China's ban.[19]

The movement of recyclable material comes at significant environmental and human cost. If we try to follow e-waste to its place of processing, this becomes clear. Many scholars and journalists have ended up at the Agbogbloshie site in Accra, Ghana, when trying to find the main global hubs for e-waste recycling and processing. There are many other sites like it across the world. For instance, journalist Fred Pearce has described the Mandoli outside New Dehli in India as a "charnel house of the digital world."[20] Although there is debate about how central the Agbogbloshie site really is,[21] we will spend some time exploring this particular site. Agbogbloshie is an area located less than a kilometer away from the Central Business District of Accra, and has an estimated population of 79,684.[22] It is in other words not a small area.

Extensive e-waste extraction takes place here. E-waste can be burned or submerged in acid to strip away unwanted material and isolate potentially valuable materials. At such sites one can see open flames and fumes, with unprotected workers performing hard physical work breaking open containers, and using acid to melt materials. Toxic materials are released in primitive recycling processes. Disposing of e-waste without recycling raises concerns about toxic health—a 2001 EPA report indicates that discarded electronics contribute approximately 70 percent of heavy metals and 40 percent of lead in US landfills—so it should not come as a surprise that toxics are released when materials are handled for recycling. These toxic materials end up poisoning the workers, who often don't wear protective equipment and don't have training to handle the risks, while others escape into the atmosphere and can come down as rain anywhere.

Agbogbloshie is both a mine and a marketplace, full of middlemen, legitimate actors, and black markets. The flow of materials in and out of the site is very dependent on commodity prices. The market is in one way abstract, a series of numbers, but it gets frighteningly concrete further down the chain. Then recovered materials get sent back up the chain, back into the global economy.

One might easily contrast the situation at sites in India, Africa, and China with high-tech e-waste recycling sites such as Skellefteå in northern Sweden. In this case, automated processes following high health and safety standards take care of the waste: "Waste heat generated during smelting is circulated to heat local buildings; and the scant leftovers from smelting are buried in purpose-built stores under the site," wrote the journalist Fred Pearce after a visit to the site.[23] Here, technology seems to have waste under control. But these sites handle only a tiny fraction of the e-waste produced.

Seen from sites like Agbogbloshie, it's not easy to say if e-waste recycling is good or not. It is a significant employment factor and revenue generator, but carrying dire environmental health risks. As geographer Ebenezer Forkuo Amankwaa argues, "the evidence so far suggests that e-waste recycling practices are not only complex, but they also manifest themselves at different scales in terms of impact on livelihood, environment and health risk."[24] It demonstrates very clearly the consequences of externalizing the cost of waste. The divide between recycling and dumping can be unclear. For instance, old computer monitors and TVs are completely unwanted, and not profitable to process because the materials in them (glass and lead) are not particularly valuable. The availability of new technologies such as flatscreens dramatically changes the economics of recycling. With TVs and monitors, the changing economics have meant that many recycling companies have simply stored the material instead of recycling it, which brings with it its own environmental costs. E-waste recyclers feel pressured to find cheaper ways to dispose of materials when the raw material prices drop. Copper, plastic, and steel values fluctuate, so when times get tough for recyclers, they make more of a profit by exporting waste than by processing it themselves.

Likewise, electronics producers also feel the pressure to reduce environmental impact of their products, and regulations like Extended Producer Responsibility makes them responsible for the cost of proper disposal at the end of a product's life. Apple provides us with one example. Driven by a wish to produce ever-sleeker and more beautiful devices, Apple's products are getting almost impossible to open, modify, or repair. According to the company's 2018 environmental responsibility report, they have countered this issue by developing a recycling robot, called Daisy, that can automatically recover valuable materials from discarded products. Eventually, the company aims to use "only recycled materials in its production processes."[25] This all sounds well and good, but the statement says nothing about it actually happening, only about the potentiality of recycling. Apple's relentless pressure to sell upgraded phones and the planned obsolescence of an industry obsessed with "innovation" make recycling promises ring hollow.

Seen from sites like Agbogbloshie, it's not easy to say if e-waste recycling is good or not. It is a significant employment factor and revenue generator, but carrying dire environmental health risks.

Electronics connect the world. But not only as a means of communications. As waste, they also connect the world. The production and the processing of waste occur in different places. Far too often we end up with what Anna Tsing has called "salvage capitalism," where (economic) value is gained through little capitalist control and regulation, where sites and resources across the world get dragged into networks of exchange and exploitation.[26]

RECYCLING BEYOND
THE HOUSEHOLD

I know that a ship is an inanimate object, but I cannot
deny that at that moment the Pioneer did die. It had
been built in Japan in 1971, and had wandered the
world under various owners and names—Cosmos Altair,
Zephyrus, Bangkok Navee, Normar Pioneer. And now,
as I stood watching from the beach, it became a ferrous
corpse—in Indian law as well as in practice no longer a
ship but just a mass of imported steel.

William Langewiesche, "The Shipbreakers"[1]

Throughout this book we have talked about the scale of
the waste problem by trying to comprehend the massive
amounts of waste. And we have seen how many forms
of regulation target producers rather than consumers
of waste. But we have not yet really tackled the issue of

industrial waste. Industrial waste by far outweighs consumer waste—and some argue against even considering consumer recycling as an effective form of environmental management. It is hard to evaluate how much industrial waste there really is, though. As we have seen, waste evades control, so nobody really knows. This makes industrial waste a particularly challenging case. This category includes not only manufacturing waste such as leftover metals, woods, and plastics; chemical solvents; paint and pigments; and sludge, but also mining waste and wastewater. Extreme amounts of matter are generated or moved around as part of the vast range of industrial processes undertaken on the Earth. Some estimates say that 97 percent of the total planetary waste stream is industrial waste, whereas only 3 percent is household waste. Is this comparing apples and oranges?

This penultimate chapter will discuss waste and recycling processes beyond the household, with the focus on industrial ecology, the dismantling of massive artifacts like ships, and the processing of mining waste. When waste is in bulk, in industrial settings, far from consumer hands or immediate concerns, we can ask whether consumers should be more concerned. Because waste processing of industrial waste has steadily been moved to developing countries in Asia and Africa, where labor is cheaper and environmental regulation less strict, this chapter will continue the previous chapter's discussion of environmental justice and the value of labor, materials, and human health.

This book has advocated for following the flow of materials across the world in assessing the concept of recycling. Within industrial production, such an approach of considering how industrial processes are connected to the world around them is often called industrial ecology. This field can be seen as response to sustainable development discourse, aiming to "make modern industrial mimic ecosystems by transforming the waste of one firm into the valuable input of another."[2] Industrial ecology was formally established following a National Academy of Sciences meeting in 1991, although the roots go back to 1960s system analysis.[3] While the field emerged out of engineering schools, it has found wider applicability since then, particularly in business schools. Business historian Christine Meisner Rosen has argued that industrial ecology as "a systems approach to thinking about the relationship between industrial activity and the natural world" could provide new directions for the way we understand the history of businesses.[4]

Industrial ecology has particularly focused on material, energy, and waste recycling among firms, in an approach that can also be termed "industrial metabolism"—where industry consumes, processes, and excretes matter just like a living organism. It is a conceptual framework that aims to connect materials and processes across industry.

In industrial processes, one often talks about "by-products" instead of waste; the output of industrial processes can often serve as a resource to be put to use in production. According to industrial ecology, everything is connected and should ideally be in balance. We saw this reflected in the LCA discussion earlier in this book. In industrial ecology, the careful use and reuse of resources is posited in contrast to a linear system of production where extraction, use, and disposal are the norm, which many practitioners and theorists argue used to be the standard approach. Such purely economically motivated systems have no "built-in tendency to recycle," argue environmental economists Pearce and Turner.[5]

In response to such a view of the industrial past, Pierre Desrochers argues that such interfirm linkages of reuse and recycling predate the contemporary discourse on industrial ecology and sustainability.[6] Just as consumer recycling is a much older phenomenon than is represented by the modern environmental framing it often gets, so are industrial recycling processes. The many examples of recycling that we have seen throughout this book also indicate that this is the case.

The industrial ecology approach dates as far back as the journalist Peter Lund Simmonds (1814–1897), who documented examples of "closed loops" in industrial settings in Victorian England, especially the recycling of animal waste. He and later industrial ecologists argued that open systems, where waste is discarded without being put to productive purposes, need to be converted into closed systems that operate more in line with natural principles of recycling. Closing the loop means that you have to place the industrial operations into a much larger system, to return to some themes we discussed earlier. Tim Cooper demonstrates how Simmonds considered waste as opportunity for "the application of technological innovations that would bring both waste matter and waste space within the confines of industrial production."[7]

Such industrial ecology approaches shape much industrial recycling today, as exemplified by the architect William McDonough's cradle-to-cradle approach.[8] Many by-products of industrial manufacturing and processing become input for new processes. One example is chemical solvents that can be processed and separated into relatively pure solvents, which also reduces the generation of hazardous waste. These solvents can be an important part of other recycling processes.

Industrial recycling patterns are shaped by economy, skills, and tools, but also by larger discursive frameworks involving societal values and priorities. We can introduce the term "waste regimes," taken from Zsuzsa Gille's study of waste management in postwar Hungary.[9] She demonstrates how both waste generation and management is, if not determined by, then definitely shaped and influenced by, sets of historical circumstances and political values.

Industrial recycling patterns are shaped by economy, skills, and tools, but also by larger discursive frameworks involving societal values and priorities.

For instance, following World War II, Hungarian recycling practices were shaped by the country's rapid industrialization, wartime destructions, and the Western embargo over precious metals that limited the country's access to virgin materials. In this context (a waste regime), waste became a "free" source of materials that could be exploited through recycling. Waste was a valuable resource that had to be surveilled and controlled by the party, like all other types of production resources. This brought with it some unintended consequences, such as that introducing waste quotas (not to limit waste, but to ensure a minimum level of waste that could be recycled) encouraged overproduction. There was also an inherent assumption that all waste was like metal scrap (practically endlessly reusable) and that long-term storage causes no environmental problems. In this waste regime, there was no emphasis on the prevention of waste generation. Problems of course arose with the chemical industry's waste, which was dramatically different from scrap metal waste. It couldn't be easily recycled or reused, and the prohibition to dump the waste in favor of storage was environmentally harmful.

Later, waste became redefined from resource to a symptom of inefficiency, where the state put more emphasis on preventing the generation of waste through increasing efficiency. But with continued economic growth, the waste problem also kept growing. Gille demonstrates how waste became redefined as a harmful material that must be dealt with through environmental technologies and dumping from the beginning of the 1980s. This shift reflected the growing significance of the chemical industry in the country and its need for assistance in dealing with nonrecyclable wastes, but also acknowledged the fledgling environmental movement that demanded safe disposal of industrial waste.

Of course, communist Hungary can be considered a relatively closed system where the input and output of materials was tightly controlled by the communist state. In the global waste economies today, the only closed system is earth itself. Power does not simply flow from above, but is distributed in formal and informal networks across the planet.

While the household recycling that we have mostly looked at so far in this book and the industrial recycling that this chapter deals with are two entirely different spheres in terms of quantity, the underlying principles of recycling are the same. What is interesting is how even the economically motivated recycling activities of industry adopted the new green rhetoric of recycling after Earth Day into their existing recycling practices. We can see this in Carl Zimring's history of the scrap metal industry, where he demonstrates how this trade set important precedents for modern recycling.[10]

We see this appear also in other areas. The scrap ship trade represents one major form of recycling metal in bulk. A modern steel ship can be a massive structure, up to 400 meters (1,312 feet). Dry cargo ships come in sizes from the small Handysize at 20,000 to 28,000 DWT (deadweight tons) up to the gigantic Chinamax-size carriers that can be 380,000 to 400,000 DWT. The size of the ships is limited by the waterways on which they have to travel and the harbors they need to visit. Like any manufactured item, ships have a lifespan, and at the end of their productive lives—on average twenty-six years—they can be recycled.[11] While many of the largest ships are made to transport iron ore across the oceans, they are also in themselves steel objects of considerable material value.

When a ship's useful life is over, it needs disposal or recycling. Shipbreaking—the full or partial dismantling of ships—is one way of reclaiming or recycling materials from the ship, which may or may not happen in a process that follows the environmental and technical guidelines published by the Basel Convention in 2003. In environmentally sound processes, ships are taken into dry docks that contain any spillage. The ship is then emptied of all fuels and hazardous materials and liquids, including the bilge water. For added safety, ventilation holes are bored so that flammable or dangerous gases can be extracted. Many ships, however, do not get dismantled according to the Basel Convention guidelines. If we go to the other extreme, ships are run ashore on beaches at high tide, so that workers can access the ship. In both cases, the ship gets stripped of everything valuable and reusable before the hull is cut up. Steel is the main material to get recycled in this process, where high-quality steel can be reused for construction (effectively downcycling it) and lower-quality steel can get melted into ingots. Ships also contain other valuable metals, such as copper used in electric cables.

Shipbreaking yards can be found on beaches across the world. Seen from above, images of such places are striking. What looks like a row of little boats on a beach fall into perspective when you notice how tiny nearby houses and roads are. Seen closer, with tiny workers holding blowtorches silhouetted against massive ships, the near-absurdity of taking apart steel ships by hand can't be denied. In many places, unprotected workers toil in heavily polluted sites under terrible conditions. Ships contain not only metal, but also fuel, oils, gases, asbestos, chemicals, and other toxic materials.

Gujarat, on the west coast of India, has been one of the world's centers for shipbreaking since the 1980s, thanks to geography, history, and cheap labor.[12] Until the 1970s, shipbreaking was not uncommon in Europe, but the introduction of more stringent health and safety laws and environmental regulations drove cost up too high. The Chinese yards on the Yangtze river are still relatively competitive with the Indian subcontinent processors, but they have been able to implement better working standards.[13] In Gujarat, the town of Alang is most important in this region, with up to 140 companies involved in ship-breaking. The work that takes place here is incredibly labor intensive and highly cost dependent. As Samantha Mac-Bride writes, "Although recycling does create jobs, the way that most recycling takes place today makes these jobs dull, hard, and harsh ones."[14]

Places like Alang "exemplify how Europe and North America have often dumped their problems on poorer places, just as their own wealthy suburbs send their garbage to poorer regions."[15] When Alang drew international attention in the 1990s after an investigation of US Naval ship scrapping, its owners defended the site from claims about terrible environmental conditions arguing that what took place there was not waste disposal, it was recycling.

Recycling has always been dependent upon labor, but with the massive scale of many industrial operations, the labor requirements are so high that recycling makes economic sense only if salaries and other expenses can be driven far enough down. Places like India and Bangladesh have become magnets for global waste owing to the low salaries and many workers willing to take jobs under almost any conditions. With this access to labor comes a tremendous ability to transform waste into value. For instance, Doron and Jeffrey tell a most fantastic story of the Indian hair trade, where individual hairs are extracted from all kinds of discarded waste materials, cleaned, sorted by length and color, and then sold in bundles that others can turn into wigs to be sold for a significant amount of money to consumers.[16] This is the essence of recycling, where a "complex chain of relationships takes the humblest of things—a single strand of discarded hair, for example—and transforms it into something of value."[17]

Shipbreaking operations seem gigantic, but they are dwarfed in comparison to mining waste, where the waste isn't just deposited in the landscape—it *is* the landscape. Mining gives us an opportunity to consider the effort necessary to reclaim and recycle valuable materials from waste at large scales. Take sites like Kiruna in Northern Sweden, where the entire city is currently being moved to give better access to one of the largest and richest concentrations of iron ore in the world. The hills surrounding the city are strangely terraced, until you realize that they are actually man-made piles of matter that has been dug up from the earth. Or take the massive open pit Bingham Canyon Mine, the largest man-made excavation in the world.[18] In mining operations, the valuable minerals extracted from the earth are interspersed with vast quantities of other matter, such as stone and soil. Separating these requires both mechanical and chemical interventions that leave behind unwanted waste such as mercury, sludge, fly-ash, and large amounts of polluted water. This waste contains potentially valuable material, and part of the cleanup process can involve reclamation and recycling of materials. For instance, the "red mud" left behind by bauxite processing contains iron, titanium, sodium, and rare earth elements, but extracting them from the toxic and alkaline red mud is not economically viable.

Since the Manhattan Project in 1942, the number of such polluted areas has grown to the thousands, ranging from very small to some of the largest concrete structures ever built. The estimated cleanup costs were enormous—at the time estimated to $200 billion—leading many to believe that the sites would never be cleaned up, effectively turning into what they called "national sacrifice zones." Like national parks, people needed to be kept out, at most being allowed to be short-term guests. But unlike a national park, it was not the land that was to be protected from people, but the people that needed to be protected from the land.

The concept "sacrifice zone" first appeared in a 1988 *New York Times* article in response to decommissioned nuclear laboratories that had become contaminated Superfund sites across the United States.[19] Sacrifice zones result from the negative impact of resource extraction on the landscape. It is easy to come up with examples—the Appalachian coalfields where strip mining and mountain top removal have devastated both landscapes and local communities; Berkeley Pit in Montana, now a toxic lake of acid; Three Gorges Dam—the world's largest power station—which displaced about 1.3 million people and flooded large areas, including valuable cultural and

Shipbreaking operations seem gigantic, but they are dwarfed in comparison to mining waste, where the waste isn't just deposited in the landscape—it *is* the landscape.

archeological sites; and the oil sands in Alberta. Deep-sea drilling and the Deepwater Horizon incident highlighted the Gulf of Mexico as sacrifice zone. There are of course sites like Chernobyl and Fukushima. And so on. Put simply, these zones are areas where resource extraction activities have damaged the environment so badly that the area must be given up as a site for human or natural presence. Historian David E. Nye calls these anti-landscapes, spaces that don't support human life.[20] We can consider these landscapes large-scale discards.

Mining waste can be mitigated in various ways, through cleanup, containment, reduction, or recycling. Mines also sit upstream of many of the processes we have explored in this book. The modern world runs on material from the extractive industries. Mining can be called unsustainable because recovery from mineral extraction involves geological processes extending over millions of years; unlike trees, ore deposits don't grow back.[21] Yet demand for minerals is increasing and existing mines cannot meet those demands. While conservation and recycling have the potential to *decrease* the demand for new mines, in the foreseeable future it will not *eliminate* the demand for new mines. Denying all mine permits because mines cannot be completely sustainable does not reduce the environmental consequences of mines; those consequences are merely shifted into regions with fewer environmental regulations. While some of this waste can be recycled in different ways, the vast majority cannot.

The legacies of mining remain for a long time after the mining activity itself has ended. In northern Sweden, for instance, there are many examples of international mining companies prospecting sites and leaving behind the waste for local authorities and residents to deal with. In recent years, such industrial activities (which also include hydropower and wind power) have been increasingly framed as a sort of resource colonialism by activists and scholars alike.[22] Max Liboiron extends such arguments in claiming that "pollution is colonialism."[23] Designating particular land areas as acceptable to pollute without the consent of the people who live there and who are affected by the environmental damage is transgression on their rights. Such processes where valuable resources are extracted from the land and where the waste is left behind can be seen as another form of separation of materials of the kind that recycling ultimately depends on. But such processes are never neutral; as Carl Zimring reminds us, waste is a product of design.[24]

IS RECYCLING GARBAGE?

Never doubt that a small group of thoughtful, committed citizens can change the world; indeed, it's the only thing that ever has.

Margaret Mead

Recycling as a conscientious action gained steam with the rise of the environmentalist movement of the 1960s. People wanted to do something for the environment, and recycling was a small-scale and locally oriented solution. Anyone could do it, without necessarily radically changing the rest of their way of life.

The green aura that recycling got in the 1970s is fading away. When recycling entered the mainstream in the late 1980s as a way for environmentally conscious Americans to reduce their waste production, journalist John Tierney was sharply critical: "The citizens of the richest society in the history of the planet suddenly became obsessed with personally handling their own waste."[1] In his view, the looming threat of the garbage crisis was overblown, an artificially produced crisis of meaning rather than a crisis of actual material things. Recycling made sense as part of an effort to preserve scarce materials, but that was no longer the case. There were other and much more efficient ways of dealing with waste. Recycling had more to do with alleviating guilt among consumers who wanted to do something for the environment; recycling became atonement rather than effective environmental action. This feeling of insufficiency is common among most who have thought critically about their own and others' recycling habits.

Recycling is a symbol, but has it become a wholly symbolic action? We have seen how scholars like Samantha MacBride and Max Liboiron are sharply critical of consumer recycling. As the former states, "Waste-oriented ecological citizens wear comfortable and increasingly sophisticated but invisible shackles that they themselves have forged in collaboration with business."[2] We have seen how business actors have embraced recycling for many different reasons, but in doing so they also adopted recycling to serve a particular agenda. The result is very often that recycling becomes a way to maintain the status quo; at best, it tries to make the most of a situation where causes seem far beyond the individual's reach, and at worst, it creates a distraction that deliberately diverts attention from

The green aura that recycling got in the 1970s is fading away.

underlying causes and shifts the focus to symptoms. The American form of environmentalism has become centered on individual responsibility, whereas in other places, recycling is mandated as a corporate responsibility. Beverage container legislation reveals this strategy clearly, as we have seen. Keep America Beautiful argued that people create waste and people can stop it, too. But what can a single individual person do in the face of the vast scale of the global waste stream? Can a person make a difference? How do we change the underlying way the world has ended up working?

Recycling is simultaneously highly symbolic and deeply material, and cannot be meaningfully reduced to either. Mirroring the waste stream it aims to extract value from, recycling is a blend of matter, politics, culture, and economics, among other things. Recycling tries to maintain a balance between hopefulness and cynicism, between environmental and economic considerations. It uncomfortably straddles the individual and the infrastructural.

This book has advocated following the materials of recycling as a way of seeing the complexity of the phenomenon. By following recycling in such a way, we can see the extent of the human footprint on earth. The world as we understand it has gotten more complex since the 1970s. In the Anthropocene, where humans have set their imprint on planet Earth down to the geological record, there is no "away" to send material to. We can follow the traces and materials of human activity to every corner of the Earth, from the highest strata of the atmosphere to the deepest oceans. In following matter, we also see that there is never just one recycling junction; there is an endless series of nodes.

The global waste problem that recycling aims to address can be called a "wicked problem." This term comes from design theorists Horst Rittel and Melvin Webber, who identified a series of characteristics of such "ill-defined" problems that "rely upon elusive political judgment for resolution."[3] Wicked problems can never really be solved, only resolved, again and again. They are unruly and muddle any attempt at defining and clarifying the parameters. There is no simple way of knowing when the problem is fully resolved, because wicked problems are also symptoms of other problems. Actual solutions require radically different societies, overthrowing the status quo.

There is no doubt that a connection exists between the aluminum can in my hand and the global environmental challenges out there, beyond the household, but connecting the dots and creating action at the individual level that has an actual impact at planetary levels is not easy. Recycling alone cannot resolve such a wicked problem; it can at best nibble away at some of the symptoms of a consumption society. But recycling can also be a way of engaging with the problem, of recognizing and considering the complexity of the situation. I do believe that many people actually want to do what is best for the environment—or at least something that is good—and the problem is not that we lack knowledge about environmental problems. Rather, people don't know how to translate this knowledge into concrete and meaningful actions. The sudden ascendancy of recycling as an environmental action from the 1970s onward can be seen as a response to this desire. It also explains the rapid adoption of recycling as a business strategy, for good and for bad.

Over the course of this book, we have seen how recycling has followed a clear trajectory from overcoming scarcity to dealing with abundance. With scarcity, recycling established a direct link, where the cause and effect of one's actions were clear. It had an immediate impact on one's own life. That is not the case in a world of abundant materials and disposables. In its contemporary form, recycling can be seen as an attempt to make the world more sustainable after the fact of overconsumption. It should be clear by now that recycling won't save the world. Let's just get that out of the way. No one single thing will.

But recycling still matters. What I see as the most significant potential of recycling is to make waste and its consequences visible. Recycling can instill a particular form of wastemindedness in its practitioners. The writer Douglas Adams famously described "something we can't see, or don't see, or our brain doesn't let us see, because we think that it's somebody else's problem."[4] As recycling has become integrated into technological systems through professionalization and institutionalization, it gradually made waste *somebody else's problem*, a problem that no longer belonged to the individual consumer that generated the waste but instead to some form of systematic waste management infrastructures. In many parts of the world, we have come to expect our waste management infrastructures to be invisible, like any other service, such as electricity. It should just work. The whole world outside the household becomes a black box that provides products and services and takes care of any waste generated. Such ignorance tends only to create more waste. The political scientist Jennifer Class has described this phenomenon as "distancing," a process that is both geographical and mental. Consumers often don't know what happens with their waste after it leaves the household, and they have little, if any, incentive or ability to significantly change the way they consume. Actors are increasingly constrained by limited choices about how to live our lives. The consumer does not act in a free setting.[5] This is the challenge of the high-tech and normalized recycling systems that many of us take for granted.

Recycling does not have to be someone else's problem, though. Recycling has the potential to serve as a vehicle for *wastemindedness*. It keeps garbage in mind. The phrase "Out of sight, out of mind" has become a truism in waste management, but the converse is also true: waste in sight, waste in mind. While the real solution to the waste problem may rest elsewhere, recycling can hold the key to keeping our attention on waste. Here we may take into consideration Noortje Marres's insights in how publics assemble around objects like waste. Such publics do not exist independently of matters of concern. These can then become political.[6] If waste is invisible and not present in our lives in one way or another, it is hard to generate public interest and concern about the larger matters that waste represents. Points of controversy and friction allow for waste to become political. In this process, we invest waste with meaning and intention. When waste management functions too well, is too effortless, too invisible or distant from the everyday, it can be hard to generate enough concern and attention to create change, as Myra Hird et al. argue. But in carefully designed systems, the attention and care for matter can become embedded in the world around us. It is a result of active choices, of politics made material.

Recycling can be a lesson in the art of attention, of noticing the many and diverse relationships between humans and waste. We can begin to ask ourselves questions: How does waste enter my household? What materials are used in the products I use and discard? Where do they come from? Where do they go once they leave my household? What can be reduced? What can be substituted with other materials? This is a form of ethnographic fieldwork,

Recycling has the potential to serve as a vehicle for *wastemindedness*. It keeps garbage in mind.

of understanding the world we live in—and ultimately, of overcoming alienation created through the disconnect between everyday lives and global processes. It is critical that this attention does not limit itself to the boundaries of the household.

Rather than considering waste as a single instance of matter that can be processed and recycled, an infrastructure perspective is useful in helping us address the cause of waste generation, and to consider waste as a holistic phenomenon. While consumer actions and values do matter, waste is ultimately generated because a manufacturer produces something, and it needs to be monitored and regulated at that level. An infrastructure perspective means another entry point for engagement. As Doron and Jeffrey have argued, technology is what mediates and mitigates the relationship between people and waste in the industrialized world.[7] Rather than engage with waste itself, we engage with the systems that generate and process waste. Rather than attempting to change consumer behavior, we are aiming to change the underlying conditions for consumer behavior.

Leaving recycling entirely to the market and its assessment of value is certainly garbage. As we know from countless examples, the market excels at generating economic value through externalizing costs, and many solutions that look cheaper or more profitable may only be so because of that. It may be cheaper to make virgin glass, but only because we don't include the environmental costs of mining sand and producing new glass (also, the world is running out of sand, believe it or not). It may be cheaper to send waste to China for processing and recycling, but that does not take into account the emissions involved in transporting the waste across the planet, or the human costs for the people who have to do the actual processing and deal with the left-behind pollution.

In a political approach to recycling, we need to address the downstreaming of environmental concerns and waste management. In recycling systems, value circulates up, but the environmental cost of recycling often cascades down in a similar fashion. It is not just different materials that get separated in recycling; economic value and environmental impact are often severed in ways that are deeply problematic. The consequences of recycling and the labor involved are not evenly distributed. Assigning proper value and costs is a political and cultural decision, where economic value and social value are intertwined.

If recycling is political, we could see recycling as citizenship, not as redemption. It is a starting point, not a goal. As with voting, it is utterly pointless as a solely individual thing. One doesn't matter, but many ones do, assuming they happen within a system that can harness and coordinate the individual actions. Recycling is not a panacea that will solve all environmental problems in the world. It might be the case that the feeling of doing something for the environment by recycling is enough to keep many from making more drastic lifestyle changes; it could equally well be that recycling makes environmental values actionable and inspires further action for many.

Tierney ends his critique of recycling on an allegorical note. In referring to Bunyan's *Pilgrim's Progress* and the appearance of a muckraker too busy taking care of his compost pile. Tierney writes, "His recycling has become the most primitive form of materialism: the worship of materials." Rather than worship, let us instead aim for attention and care for the materials that pass through our lives. Let us aim for wastemindedness. Recycling may be an imperfect solution for an imperfect world, but it is no less valuable as a point of potential environmental engagement.

Closed loop
A production system where potential waste is put back into use in production, reducing or eliminating the need for the addition of new raw materials to the system.

Compost(ing)
The biological decomposition of organic garden and food waste in order to turn it into soil conditioner.

Discard studies
A critical field of inquiry that studies waste, pollution, and externalities.

Downcycling
The reduction of value and quality in materials and products through the recycling process.

Downstream
A term that is used to direct attention to what happens with a product after it is discarded.

E-waste
Electronic waste, such as discarded TVs, telephones, computers, radios, and cables.

Greenwashing
A term that is often used about corporations and businesses that adopt a sheen of environmentalism in order to gain favor with consumers. Greenwashing typically reflects marketing practices rather than actual change in manufacturing or waste management.

Infrastructure
The underlying technological framework providing services and functionalities to a society or an organization.

Open loop
A production system where resources are "leaking out" as waste, and where new materials have to be added to the system in order for production to continue.

Upcycling
The increase of value and quality in materials and products through the recycling process. Also called creative reuse.

Upstream
A term used to direct attention to the processes that take place as part of a product's making, including the extraction of raw materials.

Waste
Discarded and unwanted material.

Waste stream
Flow of waste from its origin through to recovery, recycling, or disposal. Often used about single materials, but can also apply to particular products.

Preface

1. Ackerman 1997, 19.
2. For a good overview of discard studies, see Liboiron 2014.

Chapter 1

1. Rome 2014.
2. Anker 2007.
3. Hine 1997.
4. Dunaway 2015.
5. Anderson 1970.
6. MacBride 2012, 9.
7. European Commission 2008.
8. D Jørgensen 2014.
9. Liboiron 2014.
10. OECD 2002.
11. Cooper 2008, 710.
12. LeCain 2013, 19.
13. Offenhuber 2017, 4.
14. Melosi 1981.
15. Tarr 1996.
16. Cowan 1987; Jørgensen 2013.
17. Porter 2002.
18. Hylland Eriksen 2012, 176.
19. Seeker Stories 2015.
20. Bowker and Star 1999.
21. Tierney 1996.
22. Spelman 2016.
23. Ackerman 1997; MacBride 2012.
24. Dagens Næringsliv 2015.
25. Offenhuber 2017, 6.

Chapter 2

1. Bar-On et al. 2018.
2. Zalasiewicz et al. 2017.

3. Hawkins and Muecke 2003, xiv.
4. Doron and Jeffrey 2018, 12–13.
5. D Jørgensen 2014.
6. Clark 2007.
7. Weber 2013, 376.
8. Jørgensen 2013.
9. van der Ryn 1978.

Chapter 3
1. If you are reading this in an e-book, this exercise won't do you much good—you will have an advantage in the chapter on e-waste, though.
2. Kurlansky 2016.
3. Kurlansky 2016.
4. da Rold 2011.
5. Kwakkel 2012.
6. Lähnemann 2013.
7. O'Brien 2008, 58.
8. Kurlansky 2016.
9. Valente 2010, 6.
10. O'Brien 2008, 59.
11. Valente 2010, 8
12. Quoted in Kurlansky 2016, 219.
13. Hunter 1978.
14. McGaw 1987.
15. Strasser 1999.
16. Royte 2006, 134.
17. Ryley 2015.
18. Thorsheim 2013, 436.
19. Thorsheim 2013, 432.
20. Cooper 2008.
21. Thorsheim 2013, 435.
22. Ekheimer 2006.
23. Sjöstrand 2014, 133.
24. Sjöstrand 2014, 115.
25. Ekheimer, 87–89.
26. Royte 136.

Chapter 4
1. Toups et al. 2011.
2. Schor 2013, 35.

3. Appadurai 1986.
4. O'Brien 2008, 59.
5. Cooper 2008, 713–714.
6. Kurlansky 2016.
7. Shell 2014, 375.
8. Shell 2014, 379.
9. Jubb 1860, 43.
10. Shell 2014.
11. Jubb 1860, 2.
12. Jubb 1860, 39.
13. Jubb 1860, 55.
14. US Bureau of Labor Statistics 2006.
15. Rome 2018, 546.
16. Schor 2013.
17. Schor 2013, 34.
18. Norris 2015, 183.
19. Norris 2015, 183.
20. Norris 2015, 185.
21. Norris 2015, 186.
22. Norris 2015, 184.
23. We are following western clothes in this chapter, though Norris 2010 has also studied the flow of Indian clothing, which is no less complex than that of the West.
24. Soul Rebel Films 2012. The full documentary can be found on Vimeo and is highly recommended.
25. Norris 2015, 186.
26. Doron and Jeffrey 2018, 44.
27. Labrague 2017.
28. Labrague 2017, 181.

Chapter 5

1. Jørgensen 2013, 504.
2. FA Jørgensen 2014.
3. Friedel 2014, 507.
4. Elmore 2014, 225.
5. Hughes 1994.
6. Petersen and Arnholm 1959.
7. Packard 1960.
8. FA Jørgensen 2014.
9. Strand 2008.

10. Strand 2008, 24.
11. Dunaway 2015.
12. Elmore 2014.
13. Jørgensen 2011.
14. Doron and Jeffrey 2018, 211.
15. Doron and Jeffrey 2018, 260.
16. Alpert and O'Neill 2013.
17. Twilley 2013.
18. Norman 1988.

Chapter 6
1. Hughes 1989, 184.
2. Hughes 1987, 6.
3. Fredericks 2018, 15.
4. Fredericks 2018, 17.
5. Gendron et al. 2013.
6. Sheller 2014.
7. Royte 2006, 155.
8. Zimring 2017.
9. Sheller 2014, 17–18.
10. Also called Life Cycle Assessment.
11. Guinée et al. 2011.
12. Elmore 2017.
13. Cooper 2005, 56.
14. Jørgensen 2011.
15. Lee et al. 1995; Finnveden and Ekvall 1998.
16. Offenhuber 2017.
17. Offenhuber 2017, 81.
18. Fallan and Jørgensen 2017.
19. Gunther 2015.
20. Fallan and Jørgensen 2017, 3.
21. Chakra 2017.

Chapter 7
1. Doron and Jeffrey 2018.
2. Offenhuber 2017, 79.
3. Meikle 1995.
4. Sjöstrand 2014, 193.
5. Bach et al. 2012.

6. Wyeth 1988.
7. Hawkins 2013.
8. Hawkins 2013.
9. Elmore 2017.
10. Elmore 2014, 247.
11. Elmore 2014, 257.
12. Elmore 2014, 258–59.
13. Elmore 2017.
14. Westermann 2013, 496.
15. Jørgensen 2011.
16. Clarke 2007, 73.
17. Geyer et al. 2017.
18. Szasz 2009.
19. Chiba et al. 2018.
20. Boetzkes 2016, 51.
21. University of Bergen 2017.
22. Langston 2010.
23. Grøsvik et al. 2018.
24. Macfadyen et al. 2009.
25. Liboiron 2016, 91.
26. Liboiron 2016, 91.
27. Altman 2018.
28. Westermann 2013, 479.
29. Oldenziel and Weber 2013.
30. Westermann 2013, 481.
31. Antonelli 1995.

Chapter 8
1. Amankwaa et al. 2017, 1566.
2. Olofsson and Mali 2017, 1274.
3. Hird et al. 2014, 444.
4. Olofsson and Mali 2017, 1281.
5. Gabrys 2011; Grossman 2007; Parikka 2015.
6. Hird et al. 2014, 442.
7. Royte 2006, 171.
8. Fleming 2012.
9. Fleming 2012, 10–11.
10. Lepawsky and McNabb 2010.
11. Basel Convention 1992.

12. Grant 2016, 21.
13. Jørgensen 2011.
14. Minter 2013.
15. Lepawsky and McNabb 2010.
16. Lepawsky 2018, 70.
17. Reuters 2017.
18. Minter 2011a.
19. E-Scrap News 2017.
20. Pearce 2018.
21. Lepawsky 2018, 5.
22. Amankwaa 2013, 555–556.
23. Pearce 2018.
24. Amankwaa 2013, 572.
25. Pearce 2018.
26. Tsing 2015.

Chapter 9
1. Langewiesche 2002.
2. Desrochers 2002, 1031.
3. Desrochers 2002, 1032.
4. Rosen 1997.
5. Pearce and Turner 1990, 36.
6. Desrochers 2002.
7. Cooper 2011, 27.
8. McDonough 2002.
9. Gille 2007.
10. Zimring 209.
11. Basel Convention 2003.
12. Doron and Jeffrey 2018.
13. Minter 2011b.
14. MacBride 2012.
15. Minter 2013, 107.
16. Doron and Jeffrey 2018.
17. Doron and Jeffrey 2018, 101–102.
18. LeCain 2013.
19. Schneider 1988.
20. Nye 2013.
21. LeCain 2009.
22. Össbo 2014.

23. Forthcoming book manuscript, see also Liboiron 2017.

24. Zimring 2017, 1.

Chapter 10

1. Tierney 1996.

2. MacBride 2012, 10.

3. Rittel and Webber 1973, 160.

4. Adams 1982.

5. Clapp 2002.

6. Marres 2012.

7. Doron and Jeffrey 2018, 21.

RECOMMENDED READING

If you have made it through this book and still want to learn more about recycling, here are ten books you should read.

Ackerman, Frank. 1997. *Why Do We Recycle? Markets, Values, and Public Policy.* Washington, DC: Island Press.

Doron, Assa and Robin Jeffrey. 2018. *Waste of a Nation: Garbage and Growth in India.* Cambridge, MA: Harvard University Press.

Gille, Zsuzsa. 2007. *From the Cult of Waste to the Trash Heap of History. The Politics of Waste in Socialist and Postsocialist Hungary.* Bloomington: Indiana University Press.

Grossman, Elizabeth. 2007. *High Tech Trash: Digital Devices, Hidden Toxics, and Human Health.* Washington, DC: Shearwater.

Jørgensen, Finn Arne. 2011. *Making A Green Machine: The Infrastructure of Beverage Container Recycling.* New Brunswick, NJ: Rutgers University Press.

Lepawsky, Josh. 2018. *Reassembling Rubbish: Worlding Electronic Waste.* Cambridge: The MIT Press.

MacBride, Samantha. 2012. *Recycling Reconsidered: The Present Failure and Future Promise of Environmental Action in the United States.* Cambridge, MA: The MIT Press.

Offenhuber, Dietmar. 2017. *Waste is Information: Infrastructure Legibility and Governance.* Cambridge, MA: The MIT Press.

Strasser, Susan. 1999. *Waste and Want: A Social History of Trash.* New York: Metropolitan Books.

Zimring, Carl. 2009. *Cash for Your Trash: Scrap Recycling in America.* New Brunswick: Rutgers University Press.

REFERENCES

Ackerman, Frank. 1997. *Why Do We Recycle? Markets, Values, and Public Policy.* Washington, DC: Island Press.

Adams, Douglas. 1982. *Life, the Universe and Everything.* London: Pan Books.

Alpert, Jon, and Matthew O'Neill. 2013. *Redemption.* Video.

Altman, Rebecca. 2018. "American Beauties." *Topic Magazine* 14.

Amankwaa, Ebenezer Forkuo. 2013. "Livelihoods in Risk: Exploring Health and Environmental Implications of E-Waste Recycling as a Livelihood Strategy in Ghana." *Journal of Modern African Studies* 51 (4): 551–575.

Amankwaa, Ebenezer Forkuo, Kwame A. Adovor Tsikudo, and Jay A. Bowman. 2017. "'Away' Is a Place: The Impact of Electronic Waste Recycling on Blood Lead Levels in Ghana." *Science of the Total Environment* 601–602: 1566–1574.

Anderson, Gary. 1970. "Recycling Symbol." Museum of Modern Art. Architecture and Design Department. Object Number 137.2015.

Anker, Peder. 2007. "Graphic Language: Herbert Bayer's Environmental Design." *Environmental History* 12 (2).

Antonelli, Paola. 1995. *Mutant Materials in Contemporary Design.* New York: Museum of Modern Art.

Apparurai, Arjun. 1986. "Introduction: Commodities and the Politics of Value." In *The Social Life of Things: Commodities in Cultural Perspective*, ed. Arjun Appadurai. Cambridge: Cambridge University Press, 3–63.

Bach, Cristina, Xavier Dauchy, Marie-Christine Chagnon, and Serge Etienne. 2012. "Chemical Compounds and Toxicological Assessments of Drinking Water Stored in Polyethylene Terephthalate (PET) Bottles: A Source of Controversy Reviewed." *Water Research* 46 (3): 571–583.

Bar-On, Yinon M., Rob Phillips, and Ron Milo. 2018. "The Biomass Distribution on Earth." *Proceedings of the National Academy of Sciences*, May 2018, 201711842; DOI: 10.1073/pnas.1711842115

Basel Convention. 1992. "Parties to the Basel Convention on the Control of Transboundary Movements of Hazardous Wastes and Their Disposal." http://www.basel.int/Countries/StatusofRatifications/PartiesSignatories/tabid/4499/Default.aspx

Basel Convention. 2003. "Technical Guidelines for the Environmentally Sound Management of the Full and Partial Dismantling of Ships." Châtelaine: Secretariat of the Basel Convention.

Boetzkes, Amanda. 2016. "Plastic, Oil Culture, and the Ethics of Waste." In "Out of Sight, Out of Mind: The Politics and Culture of Waste," edited by Christof Mauch, *RCC Perspectives: Transformations in Environment and Society* 1: 51–58.

Bowker, Geoffrey, and Susan Leigh Star. 1999. *Sorting Things Out: Classification and its Consequences.* Cambridge, MA: MIT Press.

Chakra, Debbie. 2017. "Gratitude for Invisible Systems." *The Atlantic.* https://www.theatlantic.com/technology/archive/2017/05/gratitude-for-invisible-systems/526344/

Chiba, Sanae, Hideaki Saito, Ruth Fletcher, Takayuki Yogi, Makino Kayo, Shin Miyagi, Moritaka Ogido, and Katsunori Fujikura. 2018. "Human Footprint in the Abyss: 30 Year Records of Deep-Sea Plastic Debris." *Marine Policy* 96: 204–12.

Clapp, Jennifer. 2002. "The Distancing of Waste: Overconsumption in a Global Economy." In *Confronting Consumption,* edited by Thomas Princen, Michael Maniates, and Ken Conca. Cambridge, MA: MIT Press.

Clark, J. F. M. 2007. "'The Incineration of Refuse Is beautiful': Torquay and the Introduction of Municipal Refuse Destructors," *Urban History* 34 (2): 255–277.

Clarke, Tony. 2007. *Inside the Bottle: An Expose of the Bottled Water Industry.* Ottawa: Canadian Centre for Policy Alternatives.

Cooper, Timothy. 2005. "Slower Consumption Reflections on Product Life Spans and the 'Throwaway Society.'" *Journal of Industrial Archaeology* 9 (1–2): 51–67.

Cooper, Timothy. 2008. "Challenging the 'Refuse Revolution': War, Waste and the Rediscovery of Recycling, 1900–50." *Historical Research* 81 (214): 710–731.

Cooper, Timothy. 2011. "Peter Lund Simmonds and the Political Ecology of Waste Utilization in Victorian Britain," *Technology and Culture* 52 (1): 21–44.

Cowan, Ruth Schwartz. 1987. "The Consumption Junction: A Proposal for Research Strategies in the Sociology of Technology," in *The Social Construction of Technological Systems*, edited by Wiebe Bijker, Thomas Hughes, and Trevor Pinch. Cambridge: MIT Press.

Dagens Næringsliv. 2015. "Forsker: Kildesortering hjelper ikke miljøet." 7 June 2015. http://www.dn.no/nyheter/politikkSamfunn/2015/06/07/0930/forsker-kildesortering-hjelper-ikke-miljet

Desrochers, Pierre. 2002. "Industrial Ecology and the Rediscovery of Interfirm Recycling Linkages: Historical Evidence and Policy Implications," *Industrial and Corporate Change* 11 (5): 1031–1057.

Doron, Assa, and Robin Jeffrey. 2018. *Waste of a Nation: Garbage and Growth in India*. Cambridge, MA: Harvard University Press.

Dunaway, Finis. 2015. *Seeing Green: The Use and Abuse of American Environmental Images*. Chicago: University of Chicago Press.

Ekheimer, Patrik. 2006. *Tidningspapper av returpapper. Den svenska massa- och pappersindustrins omvandling under senare delen av 1900-talet*. Göteborg: Chalmers tekniska högskola.

Elmore, Bartow J. 2014. *Citizen Coke: The Making of Coca-Cola Capitalism*. New York: W. W. Norton & Co.

Elmore, Bartow J. 2017. "Plastic Bottles Are a Recycling Disaster: Coca-Cola Should Have Known Better." *The Guardian*. https://www.theguardian.com/commentisfree/2017/may/02/plastic-bottles-coca-cola-recycling-coke

E-Scrap News. 2017. "Thailand to Enact Ban on Scrap Electronics." https://resource-recycling.com/e-scrap/2018/08/23/thailand-to-enact-ban-on-scrap-electronics/

European Commission. 2008. *Directive 2008/98/EC of the European Parliament and of the Council of 19 November 2008 on Waste and Repealing Certain Directives*. Article 3. https://eur-lex.europa.eu/legal-content/EN/TXT/?uri=CELEX:32008L0098.

Fallan, Kjetil, and Finn Arne Jørgensen. 2017. "Environmental Histories of Design: Towards a New Research Agenda." *Journal of Design History* 30 (2): 103–121.

Finnveden, Göran, and Tomas Ekvall. 1998. "Life-cycle Assessment as a Decision-Support Tool: The Case of Recycling versus Incineration of Paper." *Resources, Conservation and Recycling* 24 (3–4): 235–256.

Fleming, Robin. 2012. "Recycling in Britain after the Fall of Rome's Metal Economy." *Past & Present* 217 (1): 3–45.

Fredericks, Rosalind. 2018. *Garbage Citizenship: Vital Infrastructures of Labor in Dakar, Senegal.* Durham, NC: Duke University Press.

Friedel, Robert. 2014. "American Bottles: The Road to No Return." *Environmental History* 19 (3): 502–527.

Gabrys, Jennifer. 2011. *Digital Rubbish: A Natural History of Electronics.* Minneapolis: University of Minnesota Press.

Gendron, Robin S., Mats Ingulstad, and Espen Storli, eds. 2013. *Aluminum Ore: The Political Economy of the Global Bauxite Industry.* Vancouver: University of British Columbia Press.

Geyer, Roland, Jenna R. Jambeck, and Kara Lavender Law. 2017. "Production, Use, and Fate of All Plastics Ever Made." *Science Advances* 3 (7).

Gille, Zsuzsa. 2007. *From the Cult of Waste to the Trash Heap of History. The Politics of Waste in Socialist and Postsocialist Hungary.* Bloomington: Indiana University Press.

Grant, Richard. 2016. "The 'Urban Mine' in Accra, Ghana." In "Out of Sight, Out of Mind: The Politics and Culture of Waste," edited by Christof Mauch, *RCC Perspectives: Transformations in Environment and Society* 1: 21–29.

Grossman, Elizabeth. 2007. *High Tech Trash: Digital Devices, Hidden Toxics, and Human Health.* Washington, DC: Shearwater.

Grøsvik, Bjørn E., Tatiana Prokhorova, Elena Eriksen, Pavel Krivosheya, Per A. Horneland and Dmitry Prozorkevich. 2018. "Assessment of Marine Litter in the Barents Sea, a Part of the Joint Norwegian–Russian Ecosystem Survey." *Frontiers in Marine Science* 6, March 2018. https://doi.org/10.3389/fmars.2018.00072

Guinée, Jeroen B., Reinout Heijungs, Gjalt Huppes, Alessandra Zamagni, Paolo Masoni, Roberto Buonamici, Tomas Ekvall, and Tomas Rydberg. 2011. "Life Cycle Assessment: Past, Present, and Future." *Environmental Science & Technology* 45 (1): 90–96.

Gunther, Marc. 2015. "The Good, the Bad, and the Ugly: Sustainability at Nespresso." *The Guardian.* https://www.theguardian.com/sustainable-business/2015/may/27/nespresso-sustainability-transparency-recycling-coffee-pods-values-aluminum

Hawkins, Jay, and Stephen Muecke. 2003. *Culture and Waste: The Creation and Destruction of Value.* Lanham, MD: Rowman & Littlefield Publishers.

Hawkins, Gay. 2013. "Made to Be Wasted: PET and the Topologies of Disposability." In *Accumulation: The Material Politics of Plastic,* edited by Jennifer Gabrys, Gay Hawkins, and Mike Michael. London: Routledge, 49–67.

Hine, Thomas. 1997. *The Total Package: The Secret History and Hidden Meanings of Boxes, Bottles, Cans, and Other Persuasive Containers.* Columbus, GA: Back Bay Books.

Hird, Myra, Scott Lougheed, R. Kerry Rowe, and Cassandra Kuyvenhoven. 2014. "Making Waste Management Public (or Falling Back to Sleep)." *Social Studies of Science* 44 (3): 441–465.

Hughes, Thomas P. 1987. "The Evolution of Large Technological Systems." In *The social Construction of Technological Systems. New Directions in the Sociology and History of Technology,* edited by W. E. Bijker, T. P. Hughes and T. Pinch. Cambridge, MA: MIT Press, 51–82.

Hughes, Thomas P. 1989. *American Genesis: A Century of Invention and Technological Enthusiasm, 1870–1970.* Chicago: University of Chicago Press.

Hughes, Thomas P. 1994. "Technological Momentum." In *Does Technology Drive History? The Dilemma of Technological Determinism,* edited by Merritt Roe Smith and Leo Marx. Cambridge, MA: MIT Press, 101–114.

Hunter, Dard. 1978. *Papermaking: History and Technique of an Ancient Craft.* New York: Dover Publications.

Hylland Eriksen, Thomas. 2012. *Søppel: Avfall i en verden av bivirkninger.* Oslo: Aschehoug.

Jubb, Samuel. 1860. *A History of the Shoddy Trade: Its Rise, Progress, and Present Position.* London: Houlston and Wright.

Jørgensen, Dolly. 2014. "Modernity and Medieval Muck." *Nature and Culture* 9 (3): 225–237.

Jørgensen, Finn Arne. 2011. *Making a Green Machine: The Infrastructure of Beverage Container Recycling.* New Brunswick, NJ: Rutgers University Press.

Jørgensen, Finn Arne. 2013. "Green Citizenship at the Recycling Junction: Consumers and Infrastructures for the Recycling of Packaging in Twentieth-Century Norway." *Contemporary European History* 22 (3): 499–516.

Jørgensen, Finn Arne. 2014. "Coca-Cola Bottle, USA (prototype Earl R. Dean, 1915)." In *Iconic Designs: 50 Stories about 50 things*, edited by Grace Lees-Maffei. London: Bloomsbury.

Kurlansky, Mark. 2016. *Paper: Paging Through History*. New York: W. W. Norton & Company.

Kwakkel, Erik. 2012. "Hidden Treasure, or How Destruction Creates Beautiful Things." https://medievalfragments.wordpress.com/2012/03/22/hidden-treasure-or-how-destruction-creates-beautiful-things/

Labrague, Michelle. 2017. "Patagonia: A Case Study in the Historical Development of Slow Thinking." *Journal of Design History* 30 (2): 175–191.

Lähnemann, Henrike. 2013. "Text und Textil: Die beschriebenen Pergamente in den Figurenornaten." In *Heilige Röcke: Kleider für Skulpturen in Kloster Wienhausen*, edited by Charlotte Klack-Eitzen et al. Regensburg: Schnell & Steiner, 71–78.

Langewiesche, William. 2002. "The Shipbreakers," *The Atlantic* 286 (2): 31–49.

Langston, Nancy. 2010. *Toxic Bodies: Hormone Disruptors and the Legacy of DES*. New Haven, CT: Yale University Press.

LeCain, Timothy. 2009. *Mass Destruction: The Men and Giant Mines That Wired America and Scarred the Planet*. New Brunswick, NJ: Rutgers University Press.

LeCain, Timothy James. 2013. "An Impure Nature: Memory and the Neo-Materialist Flip at America's Biggest Toxic Superfund Site." *Global Environment* 11: 16–41.

Lee, Jacquetta J., Paul O. Callaghan, and David Allen. 1995. "Critical Review of Life Cycle Analysis and Assessment Techniques and Their Application to Commercial Activities," *Resources, Conservation and Recycling* 13 (1): 37–56.

Lepawsky, Josh, and Chris McNabb. 2010. "Mapping International Flows of Electronic Waste." *Canadian Geographer* 54 (2): 177–195.

Lepawsky, Josh. 2018. *Reassembling Rubbish: Worlding Electronic Waste*. Cambridge: MIT Press.

Liboiron, Max. 2014. "Why Discard Studies." https://discardstudies.com/2014/05/07/why-discard-studies

Liboiron, Max. 2016. "Redefining Pollution and Action: The Matter of Plastics." *Journal of Material Culture* 21 (1): 91.

Liboiron, Max. 2017. "Pollution Is Colonialism." https://discardstudies.com/2017/09/01/pollution-is-colonialism/

MacBride, Samantha. 2012. *Recycling Reconsidered: The Present Failure and Future Promise of Environmental Action in the United States*. Cambridge, MA: MIT Press.

Macfadyen, Graeme, Tim Huntington, and Rod Cappell. 2009. "Abandoned, Lost or Otherwise Discarded Fishing Gear." UNEP Regional Seas Reports and Studies 185/ FAO Fisheries and Aquaculture Technical Paper 523. Rome: United Nations Environment Programme/Food and Agriculture Organization of the United Nations.

Marres, Noortje. 2012. *Material Participation: Technology, the Environment and Everyday Politics*. London: Palgrave.

McDonough, William. 2002. *Cradle to Cradle: Remaking the Way We Make Things*. New York: Farrar, Straus, and Giroux.

McGaw, Judith A. 1987. *Most Wonderful Machine: Mechanization and Social Change in Berkshire Paper Making, 1801–1885*. Princeton, NJ: Princeton University Press.

Meikle, Jeffrey. 1995. *American Plastic: A Cultural History*. New Brunswick, NJ: Rutgers University Press.

Melosi, Martin V. 1981. *Garbage in the Cities: Refuse Reform and the Environment*. Pittsburgh: University of Pittsburgh Press.

Minter, Adam. 2011a. "The Chinese Sample Room." *The Atlantic*. https://www.theatlantic.com/international/archive/2011/03/the-chinese-sample-room/72071/

Minter, Adam. 2011b. "The Shipbreakers of China," *The Atlantic*. https://www.theatlantic.com/international/archive/2011/03/the-shipbreakers-of-china/71976/

Minter, Adam. 2013. *Junkyard Planet: Travels in the Billion-Dollar Trash Trade*. New York: Bloomsbury.

Norman, Donald. 1988. *The Psychology of Everyday Things*. New York: Basic Books.

Norris, Lucy. 2010. *Recycling Indian Clothing: Global Contexts of Reuse and Value*. Bloomington: Indiana University Press.

Norris, Lucy. 2015. "Second-hand Clothing in India: The Limits of Ethicality in International Markets." *Geoforum* 67:183–193.

Nye, David. 2013. "The Anti-Landscape." In *The Anti-Landscape*, edited by David Nye and Sarah Elkind. Amsterdam: Rodopi.

O'Brien, Martin. 2008. *A Crisis of Waste? Understanding the Rubbish Society*. New York: Routledge.

OECD. 2002. *Towards Sustainable Household Consumption? Trends and Policies in OECD Countries*. Paris: OECD.

Offenhuber, Dietmar. 2017. *Waste Is Information: Infrastructure Legibility and Governance*. Cambridge, MA: MIT Press.

Oldenziel, Ruth, and Heike Weber. 2013. "Introduction: Reconsidering Recycling." *Contemporary European History* 22 (3): 347–370.

Olofsson, Jennie, and Franc Mali. 2017. "Electronic Waste: A Modern Form of Risk? On the Consequences of the Delay between the Increasing Generation of Electronic Waste and Regulations to Manage This Increase." *Human and Ecological Risk Assessment* 23 (6): 1272–1284.

Össbo, Åsa. 2014. *Nya vatten, dunkla speglingar: Industriell kolonialism genom svensk vattenkraftutbyggnad i renskötselområdet 1910–1968*. Skrifter från Centrum for samisk forskning, 19. Umeå University.

Packard, Vance. 1960. *The Waste Makers*. Philadelphia, PA: David McKay.

Parikka, Jussi. 2015. *A Geology of Media*. Minnesota: University of Minnesota Press.

Pearce, David W., and R. Kerry Turner. 1990. *Economics of Natural Resources and the Environment*. Baltimore: Johns Hopkins University Press.

Pearce, Fred. 2018. "We Know the Wrong Way to Deal with E-Waste. But What Should We Do Instead?" *Ensia Magazine*. https://ensia.com/features/e-waste/

Petersen, E. and C. J. Arnholm. 1959. *Frydenlund Bryggeri: 100 år 1859–1959*. Oslo: Frydenlund Bryggeri.

Porter, Richard C. 2002. *The Economics of Waste*. London: Routledge.

Reuters. 2017. "China Says It Won't Take Any More Foreign Garbage." https://www.reuters.com/article/us-china-environment/china-says-it-wont-take-any-more-foreign-garbage-idUSKBN1A31JI

Rittel, Horst W., and Melvin M. Webber. 1973. "Dilemmas in a General Theory of Planning." *Policy Sciences* 4 (2): 155–169

da Rold, Orietta. 2011. "Materials." In *The Production of Books in England 1350–1500*, edited by A. Gillespie and D. Wakelin, 12–33. Cambridge: Cambridge University Press.

Rome, Adam. 2014. *The Genius of Earth Day: How a 1970 Teach-In Unexpectedly Made the First Green Generation*. New York: Hill & Wang.

Rome, Adam. 2018. "Fashion Forward: Reflections on the Environmental History of Style." *Environmental History* 23 (3): 545–566.

Rosen, Christine Meisner. 1997. "Industrial Ecology and the Greening of Business History," *Business and Economic History* 26 (1): 123–137.

Royte, Elizabeth. 2006. *Garbage Land: On the Secret Trail of Trash*. New York: Back Bay Books.

Ryley, Hannah. 2015. "Waste Not, Want Not: The Sustainability of Medieval Manuscripts." *Green Letters* 19 (1): 63–74.

van der Ryn, Sim. 1978. *The Toilet Papers: Recycling Waste and Conserving Water*. Santa Barbara, CA: Capra Press.

Schor, Juliet B. 2013. "From Fast Fashion to Connected Consumption: Slowing Down the Spending Treadmill," in *Culture of the Slow: Social Deceleration in an Accelerated World*, ed. Nick Osbaldiston. London: Palgrave Macmillan.

Schneider, Keith. 1988. "Dying Nuclear Plants Give Birth to New Problems." *New York Times*, October 31.

Seeker Stories. 2015. "How This Town Produces No Trash." Video. https://www.youtube.com/watch?v=eym10GGidQU.

Shell, Hanna Rose. 2014. "Shoddy Heap: A Material History between Waste and Manufacture." *History and Technology* 30 (4): 374–394.

Sheller, Mimi. 2014. *Aluminum Dreams: The Making of Light Modernity*. Cambridge, MA: MIT Press.

Sjöstrand, Ylva S. 2014. *Stadens sopor. Tillvaratagande, förbränning och tippning i Stockholm 1900–1975*. Lund: Nordic Academic Press.

Spelman, Elizabeth. 2016. *Trash Talks: Revelations in the Rubbish*. Oxford: Oxford University Press.

Strand, Ginger. 2008. "The Crying Indian." *Orion Magazine*. November/December issue.

Strasser, Susan. 1999. *Waste and Want: A Social History of Trash*. New York: Metropolitan Books.

Soul Rebel Films. 2012. *Unravel*. Video. https://vimeo.com/193725563

Szasz, Andrew. 2009. *Shopping Our Way to Safety: How We Changed from Protecting the Environment to Protecting Ourselves*. Minneapolis: University of Minnesota Press.

Tarr, Joel. 1996. *The Search for the Ultimate Sink. Urban Pollution in Historical Perspective*. Akron: University of Akron Press.

Thorsheim, Peter. 2013. "Salvage and Destruction: The Recycling of Books and Manuscripts in Great Britain during the Second World War," *Contemporary European History* 22 (3): 431–452.

Tierney, John. 1996. "Recycling Is Garbage." *New York Times*. 30 June.

Toups, Melissa A., Andrew Kitchen, Jessica E. Light, and David L. Reed. 2011. "Origin of Clothing Lice Indicates Early Clothing Use by Anatomically Modern Humans in Africa." *Molecular Biology and Evolution* 28 (1): 29–32.

Tsing, Anna. 2015. *Mushroom at the End of the World: On the Possibility of Life in Capitalist Ruins*. Princeton: Princeton University Press.

Twilley, Nicola. 2013. "Five-Cent Redemption." *Edible Geography*. http://www.ediblegeography.com/five-cent-redemption/

University of Bergen. 2017. "Scientists Found 30 Plastic Bags in Whale's Stomach." *University Museum of Bergen*. https://www.uib.no/en/universitymuseum/104913/scientists-found-30-plastic-bags-whales-stomach

US Bureau of Labor Statistics. 2006. *100 Years of U.S. Consumer Spending: Data for the Nation, New York City, and Boston.* https://www.bls.gov/opub/uscs/report991.pdf

Valente, A. J. 2010. *Rag Paper Manufacture in the United States, 1801–1900. A History, with Directories of Mills and Owners.* Jefferson, NC: MacFarland.

Weber, Heike. 2013. "Towards 'Total' Recycling: Women, Waste and Food Waste Recovery in Germany, 1914–1939." *Contemporary European History* 22 (3): 371–397.

Westermann, Andrea. 2013. "When Consumer Citizens Spoke Up: West Germany's Early Dealings with Plastic Waste." *Contemporary European History* 22 (3): 477–498.

Wyeth, Nathaniel C. 1988. "Inventing the PET Bottle." *Research-Technology Management* 31 (4): 53–55.

Zalasiewicz, Jan, Mark Williams, Colin N Waters, Anthony D Barnosky, John Palmesino, Ann-Sofi Rönnskog, Matt Edgeworth, Cath Neal, Alejandro Cearreta, Erle C Ellis, Jacques Grinevald, Peter Haff, Juliana A Ivar do Sul, Catherine Jeandel, Reinhold Leinfelder, John R McNeill, Eric Odada, Naomi Oreskes, Simon James Price, Andrew Revkin, Will Steffen, Colin Summerhayes, Davor Vidas, Scott Wing, and Alexander P Wolfe. 2017. "Scale and Diversity of the Physical Technosphere: A geological perspective." *Anthropocene Review* 4 (1); DOI: 10.1177/2053019616677743

Zimring, Carl. 2009. *Cash for Your Trash: Scrap Recycling in America.* New Brunswick, NJ: Rutgers University Press.

Zimring, Carl. 2017. *Aluminum Upcycled. Sustainable Design in Historical Perspective.* Baltimore: Johns Hopkins University Press.

INDEX

The MIT Press Essential Knowledge Series

FINN ARNE JØRGENSEN is Professor of Environmental History at the University of Stavanger, Norway, where he is also co-director (with Dolly Jørgensen) of the environmental humanities initiative The Greenhouse. He is a historian trained in Science and Technology Studies (PhD, Trondheim, 2007) and taught as Associate Professor of History of Technology and Environment at Umeå University, Sweden, from 2010–2017. Dr. Jørgensen is the author of *Making a Green Machine: The Infrastructure of Beverage Container Recycling* and coeditor of *New Natures: Joining Environmental History with Science and Technology Studies*.